FOUNDA⁻
FOR THE FUTURE

THE FUNDRAISING ROLE OF FOUNDATION BOARDS AT PUBLIC COLLEGES AND UNIVERSITIES

MICHAEL J. WORTH

M000250137

AGB
PRESS

Foundations For The Future: The Fundraising Role of Foundation
Boards at Public Colleges and Universities

Copyright © 2012 by AGB Press

All rights reserved. No part of this publication may be reproduced or
transmitted in any form or by any means, electronic or mechanical,
including photocopying, recording, or using any information storage and
retrieval system, without permission in writing from AGB Press.

Printed and bound in the United States of America.

Library of Congress Cataloging-in-Publication Data

Worth, Michael J.

Foundations for the future : the fund raising role of foundation
boards at public colleges and universities /
Michael J. Worth.

p. cm.

ISBN 0-926508-04-0

1. Educational fund raising—United States.
2. Public universities and colleges—United States—Finance.
I. Title.

LB2336.W68 2011

379.1'30973—dc23

2011034711

For more information on AGB Press publications or to order
additional copies of this book, call 800/356-6317 or visit the AGB
Web site at *www.agb.org*.

Cover: University Hall, George Mason University, funded and built
by the George Mason University Foundation, Inc.
Photography © Eric Taylor, www.EricTaylorPhoto.com.

Association of Governing Boards
of Universities and Colleges

1133 20th Street, N.W.
Suite 300
Washington, DC 20036
www.agb.org

TABLE OF CONTENTS

FOREWORD

As the landscape of higher education continues to evolve, so too does the role of institutionally related foundations that support public colleges and universities. Once concerned primarily with receiving and stewarding philanthropic gifts on behalf of their institutions, foundations have over the last few decades become increasingly active and innovative fundraising organizations. In the face of rising costs and a prolonged economic downturn, public colleges and universities are being challenged to increase their sources of private support as state funding makes up a decreasing percentage of their budgets.

At some public institutions, foundations have already taken the lead in generating alternative sources of revenue. At others, financial pressures are only now beginning to prompt questions about whether and how their foundations should become more involved. What appears to be true across the board, however, is that the importance of private support for public institutions—and, in turn, the role of foundations—will inevitably continue to increase.

To illuminate those changes in foundation boards' fundraising duties and responsibilities, the Association of Governing Boards of Universities and Colleges (AGB) conducted a survey, in 2010, of foundation chief executive officers. Respondents answered questions such as:

- What best describes your foundation's role in fundraising? What other campus entities are involved, and to what degree?

- Who contributes gifts, how much do they contribute, and under what obligations?

- Who are the most influential groups or individuals in setting the campaign goal and priorities?

- What are the three most important practices to ensure that a foundation board is effectively engaged in fundraising?

Michael Worth—a professor of nonprofit management and former vice president for development and alumni affairs at George Washington University (and prior to that, director of development at the University of Maryland at College Park), and author or editor of nine previous books about board development, philanthropy, and fundraising—draws from the findings of the AGB survey to provide new insights into how foundation boards can improve their fundraising performance. Informed by his 30-plus years of experience in philanthropic resource development, *Foundations for the Future* is a focused look at this growing role of foundation boards and provides valuable guidance for foundation boards and their host institutions that are increasingly looking to their foundations as a source of funds.

Foundations for the Future presents a comprehensive overview of the new realities of public higher education fundraising, as well as a detailed primer on the respective roles and responsibilities of the various members of the fundraising team. Dr. Worth explains the intricacies of cultivating the fundraising capacity of a foundation board and establishing fundraising policies. He examines the role of foundation board members in giving, cultivation, solicitation, and campaigns in collaboration with the development committee, development staff, and the institution's governing board. Finally, he offers valuable best practices to help foundation boards ask the right questions, set appropriate goals, and do their utmost for the institutions they serve.

For more than two decades, AGB has recognized and supported the growing impact of foundations and their boards on public colleges and universities, and the necessity of the collaborative relationship between the foundation and the institutions they support. During this period of financial constraints, when the relationship between a foundation and its host institution needs clarity and collaboration, AGB continues to expand its programs and services for foundations. This new book is the latest addition to AGB's ongoing study and development of board practices in leading these complex organizations.

We are pleased to offer this timely and practical guide for board leaders and other fundraising professionals. *Foundations for the Future* is essential reading for directors of institutionally related foundations, foundation executives, institution and system chief executive officers, chief advancement officers, academic officers who work with institutionally related foundations, and governing board members of public institutions.

Richard D. Legon
President
Association of Governing Boards of Universities and Colleges
December 2011

PREFACE

Twenty-eight years ago I completed a Ph.D. in higher education at the University of Maryland. My dissertation concerned the relationships between the governing boards of public universities and the boards of their institutionally related foundations. It was an early study on a topic that had not received much attention before; my literature review uncovered only one other dissertation that had addressed it at the time. That finding was not surprising. In the 1980s, the existence of institutionally related foundations was a relatively new phenomenon at many public institutions, with the exception of state universities in the Midwest and some in the Mid-Atlantic, at which they had long existed.

Among the members of my dissertation committee was Richard T. Ingram, then executive vice president of the Association of Governing Boards of Universities and Colleges. The fact that AGB was interested in these foundations and their boards at that time is testimony to the association's tradition of alertness to emerging trends in higher education, and its interest has been justified by the enormous growth in the number and scale of such foundations in subsequent decades.

Since that first experience with AGB as a graduate student, I have worked with the association on two other projects. The first, a study in 2004 that examined the fundraising roles and responsibilities of boards of trustees at independent colleges and universities, resulted in a small book published by AGB in 2005: *Securing the Future: A Fundraising Guide for Boards of Independent Colleges and Universities.* A few years later, AGB and I collaborated on a study of advisory councils in higher education, at both independent and public institutions. AGB published *Sounding Boards: Advisory Councils in Higher Education* in 2008. The book encompassed my summary and reflections on AGB's research. In the context of this long relationship, I was enthusiastic when Richard D. Legon, AGB's president, suggested in 2010 that we make it a trilogy, by cooperating in a study of the fundraising roles and activities of the boards of institutionally related foundations. Findings from that study are woven throughout this volume.

It is important to emphasize that this book, and the research on which it is based, are intended to be narrow in scope. This is not a book that deals with the subject of institutionally related foundations comprehensively or that is intended to address broad issues related to the governance of such foundations. The 2010 AGB survey did not attempt to compile exhaustive data about the operations of foundations or their work in managing funds and other activities on behalf of their institutions. The focus of the study and this book is specifically on the roles and responsibilities of foundation boards in *fundraising*.

As discussed further in Chapter 1, many institutionally related foundations began as passive entities that received and managed private support for the benefit of public colleges and universities. An active leadership role in fundraising for their institutions is a relatively new role for some of them, and some foundation boards are grappling with the transition. With declining state support for public higher education, active fundraising foundations may become essential to maintaining the quality of public higher education in the future, a goal of utmost importance to the vast majority of Americans who receive their education at these institutions and to the nation as a whole.

It is my hope that this book will provide useful information and insights for foundation directors and foundation chief executive officers, as well as presidents and board members of public institutions who are seeking the most effective ways of serving their institutions.

Michael J. Worth
Washington, D.C.
December 2011

ACKNOWLEDGMENTS

I am grateful to Richard D. Legon, AGB's president, and Susan Whealler Johnston, executive vice president, who encouraged and supported this writing and the research on which it is based. Having worked with both of them on previous AGB projects, I appreciate their continued confidence in me as an AGB author.

I also express thanks to David G. Bass, AGB's director of foundation programs and research, and Marla B. Bobowick, director of AGB Press, who guided the 2010 AGB survey and the development of this publication. I am grateful as well to Colin Welch, my graduate assistant at George Washington University, and to Philip E. Bakerman, research assistant at AGB, who provided valuable assistance in organizing and interpreting data from AGB's 2010 survey of foundation chief executive officers.

And, of course, I appreciate the time and effort of the foundation chief executive officers who responded to AGB's survey and am especially grateful to those who permitted me to interview them in connection with the brief case studies that are included in this book.

CHAPTER 1

A CHANGING LANDSCAPE FOR PUBLIC HIGHER EDUCATION

I n the fall of 1977, I arrived at the University of Maryland College Park to start my new job in a recently created position called "director of development." A small development office was already based in the university system office, which provided some services to five campuses. On the College Park campus, an existing fundraising operation was associated with the athletics department, and two of the professional schools had assistant deans whose responsibilities included fundraising to some extent. But there was no campuswide coordination of efforts. It would be an understatement to say that the culture was not fully supportive of organized fundraising. Indeed, I learned—after I arrived—that some campus administrators, who thought the salary would not be justified by the slim possibility of raising significant private money, had been opposed to the creation of my position.

I had no staff and controlled few resources, except for small amounts carved from the overall communications budget. I had to be careful not only about how much was spent, but on what—for example, no alcohol. Any gifts to the campus were deposited in state accounts, requiring a cumbersome process to expend. Over my several years at Maryland, the university created an institutionally related foundation, put in place the building blocks of a comprehensive fundraising program, and successfully complete some focused campaigns that began to establish a culture of philanthropy. But by the early 1980s, when I left College Park to become vice president for development and alumni affairs at George Washington University, Maryland's development program was still in its infancy.

The situation at that time at most other public institutions was not that different. Public universities in the Midwest already had long-established traditions of raising funds from alumni and other private sources, as had some institutions in the Mid-Atlantic region, notably the University of Virginia and the University of North Carolina at Chapel Hill. The first university-related foundation, the Kansas University Endowment Association, had been created in 1891. But in the 1970s, in most states, public colleges and universities were, in fact and in perception, agencies of state government. They received most of their

TAKEAWAYS FOR FOUNDATION BOARD MEMBERS

- With reduced state appropriations, philanthropic support for core operating budgets has become a high priority for public institutions of all types. In fact, the campaign goals of many public research universities now equal or exceed those of their independent counterparts.

- Public institutions facing the need for increased private support have established institutionally related foundations, and the fundraising role of foundation boards is of growing importance.

- An institutionally related foundation can generate funds for investment in fundraising programs, help ensure the proper management of gifts, and provide greater flexibility in investing funds.

- A foundation board should be constructed in a way that is consistent with the foundation's overall fundraising strategy, and board members should be selected at least in part for their ability to provide or obtain private support.

- A recent AGB study of foundations found that the most common pattern is for the foundation board to participate in cultivation, solicitation, and stewardship activities, accompanied by the resident or development office or foundation staff members.

- Most institutions include members of the foundation board in leadership committees for capital campaigns.

support from the legislature, had low tuition, and did not raise gift support in a purposeful manner.

Today, more than 30 years later, the situation is vastly different. In response to a new financial landscape, private support is now central to colleges' and universities' aspirations for the future and increasingly important even to meet current operating needs.

Boards of public colleges and universities, however, have not typically been viewed as sources of such support—either of giving money or raising it—for the institutions that they govern. Most boards of public institutions are appointed by political officials, usually the governor with confirmation by the legislature, or elected by alumni or the public. Unless members are appointed by a governor who happens to place a high priority on private support, it is unlikely that a public governing board will be well-situated to play a leadership role in fundraising for the institution. Such boards include many talented people who work tirelessly in meeting their responsibility to ensure that public funds are properly applied and that the college or university serves the public purposes for which it exists. But the process by which public governing boards are appointed does not ensure that the board will include individuals of affluence or influence, leaders from the business community, or prominent and successful alumni who live outside the state.

It is for this reason, among others, that public institutions facing the need for increased private support have established institutionally related foundations. The fundraising role of foundation boards is thus a subject of growing interest and importance, and it is the focus of this book.

As a private entity, an institutionally related foundation has a board with the ability to define and design its own membership, much like the board of an independent college or university. Some members will be selected for their expertise in managing investments and real estate—important aspects of many foundations' activities—but many will be selected for their ability to provide or obtain private support. They will include wealthy individuals as well as members who have access to philanthropy, perhaps as representatives of corporations or foundations that support higher education. The board may also enlist new members to provide leadership in various cities or professions or to ensure that alumni of various programs are represented.

In other words, the board can be constructed in a way that is consistent with the foundation's overall fundraising strategy. And, as the rest of this book will make clear, having a board positioned to play its role as part of the fundraising team is essential to achieving success in securing philanthropic support. Among others, this book addresses such questions as:

- What role do foundation boards play in giving and fundraising for their institutions in ongoing programs and, especially, during a campaign?
- What are the respective roles of foundation board members, institutional governing board members, institutional presidents or chancellors, and advancement professionals as members of the fundraising team?
- Who makes decisions about fundraising goals and priorities and the metrics by which fundraising performance is evaluated?
- How do foundation boards and institutional governing boards coordinate with regard to fundraising goals and policies?
- How effectively are foundation boards meeting the increasing expectations that public colleges and universities hold for them?
- And, finally, what are some best practices that foundation boards should consider with regard to their fundraising role?

AN EVOLVING CASE FOR SUPPORT

As a fundraiser for a public university in the late 1970s and early 1980s, I sometimes would be asked, "Why should I give the university more money; isn't it already funded with my tax dollars?" An answer to that question had been formulated in the mid-1960s, although it took time to gain broad understanding. A statement entitled "Margin for Excellence: The Role of Voluntary Support in Public Higher Education," published in 1966 by the voluntary support committee of the National Association of State Universities and Land Grant Colleges (now the Association of Public and Land-Grant Universities), provided a simple but persuasive rationale for private support of public higher education and laid the groundwork for increasing philanthropy in the years ahead. It read:

> Tax funds generally can support the basic needs of public higher education.
> But the ingredients for academic excellence include private support.

Tax revenue can be used to build and maintain most classrooms, libraries, and laboratories. They can provide average salaries for faculty members. But then there are all the enriching features of a sound educational program that mean the difference between good and great universities: new and challenging courses of study, cultural programs, museum and library collections, continuing research, unusual equipment, student aid, competitive faculty salaries, special buildings.

These represent the "margin for excellence," which depends chiefly on private support.

Why should public colleges and universities develop this margin for excellence? The answer is not a selfish one: The progress of the entire nation is at stake.

That statement had all the attributes of a sound and succinct case for support. It assured donors that private support was needed, that it would supplement rather than supplant public funds, and it made the connection between excellence in public higher education and the broader well-being of the nation. The creation of this statement was a great contribution to the cause, and the margin-for-excellence theme remained at the core of the case for private support of public colleges and universities in the following decades. And, over the years, it gained increasing recognition and acceptance among donors.

Today the case for private support of public higher education has expanded. The margin-for-excellence approach is still relevant, but with reduced state support, philanthropy has become an essential component of core funding for some public institutions. And philanthropy is likely to become even more crucial to public colleges and universities in the future.

FROM STATE-SUPPORTED TO STATE-LOCATED

The recession that began in 2007 and its aftermath brought state budget crises of a magnitude unseen since the Great Depression. This resulted in major cuts in state funding for higher education. Reductions in state appropriations were accompanied by significant tuition increases and other adjustments. Forty-three states made budget reductions and/or increased tuition in 2010-11, but the changes were most dramatic in the states that were hardest hit by the recession. According to a 2010 report, written by Nicholas Johnson, Phil Oliff, and Erica Williams and posted on the Web site of the Center for Budget and Policy Priorities, Florida public institutions increased tuition by a total of 32 percent over the 2009-10 and 2010-11 academic years. The University of California raised tuition by 32 percent and reduced freshman enrollment by 2,300 students. The California State University System cut enrollment by 40,000. Even Texas, with an economy that weathered the recession relatively well, slashed higher education funding by 5 percent, a drop of $73 million. By 2010, some observers were describing a "new normal" and predicting that state support for higher education would never return to pre-recession levels on a per-student basis.

But the transformation of public higher education finance did not begin in 2007; it has been going on for decades. State appropriations for higher education have risen and fallen with economic cycles, but over the long term, they have not kept pace with enrollment growth and inflation. Data from "State Higher Education Finance, 2009," published by the State Higher Education Executive Officers, describe the trends. Per-student appropriations rose to a high of $7,961 in 2001. They plummeted in the next three years, recovered to $7,220 by 2006, and then dropped again to $6,928 in 2009. State funding per student, adjusting for inflation, was lower in 2009 than in most years since 1980. At the same time, net tuition revenue (excluding student aid, discounts, and so forth) grew from 25 percent of total educational revenue (excluding debt service) in 1984 to 37 percent by 2009. In other words, over the past three decades, the burden of paying for higher education generally has shifted from taxpayers to students and their families.

The relative decline in state support for public higher education reflects in part the competing demands on state budgets, including prisons, health care, and infrastructure. For example, according to an article by John Pulley in the July/August 2010 issue of *Currents*, the budget of the University of California increased 2 percent from 2000 to 2010, while the state's health care costs went up 47 percent, K-12 budgets jumped 43 percent, and state funding for the corrections system more than doubled.

There also has been a change in the nation's philosophy regarding higher education. Beginning in the mid-19th century it came to be viewed as a public good, like K-12 education, roads, and parks—of benefit to all people and thus worthy of public funding. The public investment in colleges and universities was justified by the benefits of an educated population to all of society, including the potential impact on the economic development of states. That justification still exists, but now many people, including some state legislators, tend to regard higher education more as a private good. The benefits of a college degree include higher earnings over an individual's lifetime; education is thus an investment by that individual and his or her family that provides a significant financial return. Those who view higher education in this way can then conclude that the costs should be paid primarily by the individuals who benefit, and perhaps by donors, with the state's financial contribution becoming more limited. Thus, philosophy as well as economics has contributed to the transition in the financing of public colleges and universities.

For some public research universities, state funds have become a relatively small slice of the pie, and the impact of tuition and gifts now exceeds that of appropriated funds. For example, in 2008-09, the state appropriation to the University of Virginia provided just 8.2 percent of the university's overall revenue, according to a report entitled "Funding the University 2008-09: A Public-Private Partnership," posted on the university's Web site. That was less than the 9.1 percent coming from gifts and endowment and the 16.2 percent derived from tuition and fees. A 2009 article by Nancy Folbre in the *New York Times* quotes James J. Duderstadt, the former president of the University of Michigan, who describes the shifting patterns: "We used to be state-supported, then state-assisted, and now we are state-located." (The quotation has been attributed to—and spoken by—many different people. It is now so well-known that some articles refer to it merely as "the old line about....") It is, of course, important to note that while this scenario exists at some research universities, public funds still provide the overwhelming share of total revenue at most public master's, baccalaureate, and two-year institutions.

As the slices of the revenue pie have changed, flagship campuses in Virginia, Michigan, and other states have privatized some professional schools, forgoing state funds for the freedom to set tuition levels and increase the enrollment of out-of-state students. Some public institutions have adopted a version of the high-tuition/high-aid strategy long followed by independent colleges and universities, increasing the posted tuition toward market levels while offering financial aid to students based on need. In many cases, tuition increases have been accompanied by the elevation of scholarship support to the highest priority for fundraising.

The new reality has brought forth debate and proposals for broader reform in public higher education finance, some of which are summarized by James Garland in the July/August 2010 issue of *Currents*. Some people advocate shifting state funding from institutions toward subsidies of students, who then could take their state-supported scholarship funds to the institutions that most attract them, whether independent or public. There are calls for campuses to reduce their operating costs through greater efficiency and to do a better job of measuring results so that scarce resources can be allocated to the most-productive programs. As reported in the March 4, 2011 *Chronicle of Higher Education*, some state legislators have advocated more restrictions on public institutions, including limits on faculty salaries, sabbaticals, and unions. Others have called for further deregulation of public colleges and universities, perhaps converting them to quasi-public entities with independent governing boards and the power to set their own admission standards, curricula, salaries, and tuition and fees—much like independent institutions.

Whatever new approaches or models may be adopted, it is clear that philanthropic support has become a high priority for public institutions of all types. As Dave Frohnmayer, president of the University of Oregon, wrote in the September/October 2006 issue of *Trusteeship*:

> When have you last seen a new president at a public university not initiate a fundraising drive to implement a new "strategic vision," with new talk about public-private partnerships? Every public university in America is planning for, in the midst of, or emerging from (which is code for "planning for") a fundraising campaign. That is relatively new in the public sector. For many stakeholders, including faculty and sometimes even legislators, it is rapidly becoming a major measure of a president."

GROWING PRIVATE SUPPORT

Philanthropic support for higher education grew over the decade of the 2000s, despite economic and market volatility, and public institutions did gain ground. According to the *Voluntary Support of Education* survey, published by the Council for Aid to Education, private gifts to higher education in 2000 totaled $19.4 billion, including $8.3 billion (43 percent) going to public colleges and universities. According to the same survey, by 2009—a year in which overall giving to higher education dropped by more than 11 percent—public institutions received more than $11 billion in philanthropy, about 46 percent of the total. As shown in Table 1.1, of the 20 institutions receiving the highest total of voluntary support in 2010, eight were public.

Table 1.1 – Top 20 Institutions by Voluntary Support, 2010

Institution	Voluntary Support, 2010
1. Stanford University	$598,890,327
2. Harvard University	$596,963,000
3. Johns Hopkins University	$427,593,283
4. University of Southern California	$426,016,332
5. Columbia University	$402,356,576
6. University of Pennsylvania	$381,591,586
7. Yale University	$380,903,371
8. New York University	$349,213,948
9. Duke University	$345,468,017
10. Indiana University	$342,818,089
11. University of California, Los Angeles	$340,406,763
12. University of Wisconsin-Madison	$311,846,992

13. Cornell University	$308,219,446
14. University of California, Berkeley	$307,509,066
15. Massachusetts Institute of Technology	$307,181,598
16. University of Washington	$285,219,625
17. University of California, San Francisco	$268,904,940
18. University of North Carolina at Chapel Hill	$266,857,424
19. University of Michigan	$252,098,059
20. University of Chicago	$251,233,491

Source: Council for Aid to Education Web site, accessed March 2, 2011 (http://www.cae.org/content/pdf/ Top_Twenty_and_By_State_2010.pdf)

In the beginning of this chapter, I described the low priority given to fundraising at the University of Maryland when I served there in the 1980s. Providing a striking example of how things have changed, by 2010 Maryland was among a number of public universities conducting campaigns with goals of $1 billion or more. Indeed, the campaign goals of many public research universities now equal or exceed those of their private counterparts. For example, an update on continuing campaigns in the June 7, 2010 *Chronicle of Higher Education* listed a goal of $4 billion at Cornell University, followed by goals of $3 billion at the University of Virginia, the University of California at Berkeley, and the University of Texas at Austin. At $2 billion, Penn State's campaign goal was somewhat larger than Vanderbilt's ($1.75 billion), Princeton's ($1.75 billion), and Emory's ($1.6 billion).

Again, however, it is important to disaggregate the data. Of the $11 billion given to public higher education in 2009, over $9 billion went to research/doctoral universities, an increase over the $7 billion received by those institutions in 2000. Private support of master's, baccalaureate, and two-year public institutions still remains a relatively small percentage of total higher education philanthropy and of those institutions' operating budgets. It is also essential to bear in mind that many gifts are restricted to a specific purpose or program and thus may not provide support to core operating budgets or the discretion to allocate the funds to areas most in need of funding. For that reason, for most institutions, philanthropy simply does not provide a complete substitute for state funds or tuition revenue.

Campaign goals also reflect the philanthropic predominance of research universities. The Council for Advancement and Support of Education's (CASE) *2007 Campaign Report* revealed that the median campaign goal at both independent and public research/doctoral institutions was $500 million. Again including both the independent and public sectors, the median campaign goal for master's institutions was $42.5 million; for baccalaureate institutions, it was $65 million. For two-year institutions, most of which are public community colleges, the median campaign had a goal of just $16.4 million. Despite growth in private support, public colleges and universities continue to face a fundraising gap with their independent counterparts. For example, a 2009 study conducted by Peter B. Wylie and John Sammis, reported by Diane Webber Thrush in *Currents* (July/August 2010), found that the top 5 percent of donors at the average independent institution had given a lifetime total of at least $3,000, compared with an average of $450 for alumni of public colleges and universities. Alumni participation—that is, the percentage of alumni who make any gift in a given year—generally averages less than 10 percent at public institutions, while rates as high as 40 percent are found at some institutions in the independent sector.

To some extent, the differences are attributable to demographics and arithmetic. Many public institutions have larger and more economically diverse alumni bodies than independent colleges and universities do, making it more difficult to increase average gifts and alumni participation rates. The denominator is just so large that even a substantial increase in the numerator—that is, the number of donors—has little impact on the rate. And, although the case for private support is better understood today than in past decades, some donors still may question the need for giving to what they perceive to be state-supported entities.

But major campaigns at public institutions have become more common beyond the flagship campuses—including, for example, in 2010, ongoing efforts at Oregon State ($625 million goal), Western Kentucky University ($200 million goal), and the University of Texas at El Paso ($180 million goal). And although they are relative newcomers to organized fundraising, community colleges have begun to mount significant campaigns. For example, in 2008 the 110 community colleges in California launched a combined campaign to raise $50 million in endowment for scholarships by 2011. Reflecting the growing focus on private support among its members, the American Association of Community Colleges (AACC) launched a new Web site in September 2010 dedicated to fundraising resources for its presidents.

FOUNDATIONS FOR THE FUTURE

As mentioned previously, the first university-related foundation was the Kansas University Endowment Association, founded in 1891 as an independent 501(c)(3) organization, "for the purpose of receiving, managing, and administering money and other gifts for the use and benefit of the University of Kansas." It is instructive that the word "raising" was not included. The founders' goal was to find a solution to a specific problem. The university had been offered an opportunity to purchase land at a very attractive price and wanted to use a previous cash gift for the purchase. But state law required that any gifts to the university be deposited in a state general fund, with interest from the fund going to benefit all the state's universities. Private dollars were essentially treated the same as tax dollars, with the same requirements on their use. By creating the endowment association (foundation) as a separate, private legal entity, its founders were able to receive gifts and make investments for the specific benefit of the University of Kansas.

In other words, the first foundation—like many that followed—was what Joseph F. Phelan called, in *College & University Foundations: Serving America's Public Higher Education* (AGB, 1997), a "passive repository." Its purposes were to keep private funds separate from the state treasury, to allow the university to own and manage assets with flexibility that state law did not provide the university itself, and to assure that gifted assets would be directed toward the particular institution and purposes that donors might have designated. The idea that foundations might be active fundraising entities came later.

BENEFITS OF AN INSTITUTIONALLY RELATED FOUNDATION

Some public colleges and universities can and do raise and manage private funds within the structure of the institution itself. Their ability to do so and the flexibility with which they can use private gifts vary from state to state. But an institutionally related foundation offers several advantages that have led to their growth in recent decades, including:

- *A foundation signifies a long-term commitment to the pursuit of private support.* The term "foundation" is well-recognized and connotes both "private" and "permanent." The fact that a college or university has created a foundation sends a message that private support is a high priority and brings distinct visibility to fundraising efforts. Since the leadership of the institution itself may change over time, the foundation's board and staff may provide greater continuity in maintaining relationships with donors and sustaining fundraising efforts during transitions in institutional leadership.

- *A foundation can generate funds for investment in fundraising programs.* The ability of public institutions to spend money on fundraising varies among the states, and fluctuations in institutional budgets over the economic cycle work against a sustained effort. Although a foundation's resources also vary with economic cycles, and many were forced to reduce staffing during the 2007-09 recession, it may enjoy more options. Foundations have developed a variety of mechanisms, including fees and income earned on gifts, to provide the staff and other resources necessary to sustain an ongoing fundraising effort.

- *A foundation can help ensure the proper management of gifts.* Thousands of gifts may be received each year and many may be designated for very specific purposes. Properly acknowledging the gifts and maintaining the accounting required to ensure that donor directions are followed is a specialized task. The campus-based financial office may not have the skills or systems to accomplish it and, if private support is a relatively small portion of total revenue, may not devote its full attention to this area. By combining gift management and stewardship within a single entity, a foundation can focus its full-time attention on the application of gifts to their intended purposes and close the loop through reporting to the donors.

- *A foundation has more flexibility in investing funds.* Public institutions and their governing boards are often constrained from adopting investment policies that may involve risk and may not be able to quickly accept or dispose of unusual assets. As a private entity, the foundation can take a long-term perspective, allocate investments to ensure the greatest return over time, and invest in a wider array of assets. A foundation also can manage planned gifts, such as charitable remainder trusts and charitable gift annuities, which might be difficult or impossible for a public institution to handle directly. Some foundations have become the entrepreneurial arms of their institutions, engaging in partnerships with business and developing and managing real estate, with the flexibility of a private entity that a public college or university itself would not be able to achieve.

- *A foundation offers an opportunity to create a self-perpetuating board.* From the fundraising perspective, one of the greatest advantages of a foundation is the chance to create a board that is designed, at least in large part, to be effective in raising private support. In other words, it provides a way to deal with the separation between governing and fundraising that has been one of the reasons for the gap between independent and public institutions in philanthropic support. While the governing board of the college or university retains legal authority and responsibility for the institution's policies and programs, the foundation board has responsibility for the funds that it raises and manages. Serving on such a board is thus a more substantive assignment than participating as a member of an advisory council that has no formal responsibilities. The foundation-board position thus may be particularly attractive to accomplished individuals who wish to be associated with a college or university.

FOUNDATIONS AND THEIR INSTITUTIONS

Although institutionally related foundations are, by definition, separate legal entities with boards that are distinct from the institutions' governing boards, the relationship between an institutionally related foundation and the college or university may be complex. There are three basic models.

In a 2010 survey of foundation chief executive officers conducted by the Association of Governing Boards of Universities and Colleges (referred to simply as the "2010 AGB survey" throughout this book), 19 percent of foundations identified themselves as *dependent*. These foundations essentially function as a unit of the institution, which provides office space, staff, and other support. This is the situation for most foundations that are passive recipients of private gifts.

Another 53 percent of foundations participating in the 2010 AGB survey are *interdependent*. They receive some free in-kind benefits from their institutions, such as office space or the services of institutional staff, but also generate some of their own operating budgets.

In the 2010 AGB survey, 29 percent of foundations described themselves as *independent*. These foundations operate with a high degree of autonomy, usually employ at least some of their own staff, and reimburse the institution for any use of institutional resources by the foundation. There also appears to be a correlation between endowment size and the degree of the foundation's independence. Two different AGB studies—one in 2007 and the other in 2010—found that half of foundations with endowments over $100 million described themselves as independent. Independence also is more common among foundations that have existed for a long time.

It must be noted that some foundations support systems of public institutions and that some are affiliated with individual colleges or schools within a larger institution. The 2010 AGB survey included only a small number of such foundations; they are important, but are they are not a significant focus in this book.

The position of foundation chief executive officer mirrors the varied relationships that foundations have with their institutions. In the 2010 AGB survey, 52 percent of foundation executives were also officers of their institutions, typically a vice president, while 48 percent were not officers of their institutions. Of those foundation CEOs who responded to AGB's survey, 34 percent report only to the foundation's board; 38 percent report to both the foundation board and the institution's president or chancellor; 7 percent report to the foundation board and another institutional officer (for example, a vice president for advancement); 21 percent report only to the institution's president or chancellor; and fewer than 1 percent report only to an institutional officer other than the president—for example, to a vice president for advancement.

The compensation of foundation chief executives also reflects diverse practices. In 2010, according to the AGB survey, 37 percent were paid only by the foundation, 42 percent were paid only by the institution, and 21 percent were paid by both the foundation and the institution. As these patterns clearly suggest, the job of a foundation chief executive officer is one that requires a high level of political judgment and communications ability.

Cause for Controversy

Relationships between institutions and their related foundations sometimes have been the source of controversy. Some cases have involved personalities; others have reflected unethical behavior or mismanagement. But the potential for conflict is inherent in the institution-foundation relationship. And the changing financial landscape described above may increase that potential in the years ahead.

In a December 2008 article in *Trusteeship*, David G. Bass, director of foundation programs and research at AGB, and James L. Lanier, former president, CEO, and vice chancellor for institutional advancement at the East Carolina University Foundation and the ECU Real Estate Foundation, identify four factors that have caused institutionally related foundations to become involved in controversy:

- Demands by donors and constituents within the affiliated institutions for greater accountability and transparency in the use of gifts;
- Heightened governance and compliance standards for both foundations and institutions;
- The growing complexity of financial functions and asset management, as well as the increasing scale of fundraising campaigns; and
- A greater number of foundation chief executives being drawn from outside of higher education, who may not be familiar with the distinct higher education culture.

NEW DEMANDS, NEW PRESSURES

As I discussed above, public higher education institutions are facing significant financial constraints. Their presidents and governing boards are exploring every opportunity for enhanced revenue, and that may translate into pressure on foundations—both to raise more unrestricted funds and to increase the payout rate on foundation-held endowments. Indeed, as David G. Bass, director of foundation programs at AGB, and James L. Lanier, former president, CEO, and vice chancellor for institutional advancement at the East Carolina University Foundation and the ECU Real Estate Foundation, describe, there have been legislative proposals to impose a minimum payout rate on institutional endowments and institutionally related foundations—in other words, to subject them to the type of requirement that now applies to private foundations. Such legislative proposals are based on the argument that higher education foundations may not be providing a public benefit commensurate with the tax advantages they enjoy. But the new financial landscape for public higher education may play a role as well. Some state legislators, and perhaps some institution presidents and governing boards, might favor a greater payout from foundations to replace declining revenue from other sources.

At the same time, foundation boards have a fiduciary responsibility to donors to ensure that any restrictions on their gifts are honored and that endowment funds are invested to maintain purchasing power in the face of inflation. The latter may require a conservative approach to endowment payouts, especially at times when the markets have declined. Of course, these are also the times when state funding is likely to decline and institutions need more revenue from private sources. As Bass and Lanier point out in their December 2008 article in *Trusteeship*, the foundation's responsibility to donors also may sometimes place foundations in the position of enforcer and auditor of the institution—a role that may not be fully appreciated by cash-strapped presidents and governing boards.

As Bass and Lanier note, in recent years the Internal Revenue Service has increased its scrutiny of higher education generally and has sought to "map the interrelated financial operations and governance practices of institutions and all their affiliated organizations." Again, the emphasis on accountability and transparency is likely to raise issues about who should control the use of foundation resources, possibly causing tension between foundation boards and institutional governing boards.

When private support provided only the margin for excellence, gifts often supported the construction of buildings, the creation of endowment for scholarships or professorships, and other purposes that were add-ons to what was available through core state support. Surely there were instances in which donors provided funds for purposes that may not have been the highest priority of institutional leaders or governing boards, but as long as gifts supported acceptable purposes and did not impose too much additional cost on the institution, there was no reason not to welcome the support and little cause to view the foundation as intruding on institutional decision making.

But there is now increasing pressure on foundations to go beyond the margin-for-excellence approach and respond to the need to raise more unrestricted support for institutions' core operating budgets. As Richard D. Legon, president of AGB, observes in the 2005 book *Margin of Excellence*, the increased role of foundations in providing operating funds may cause concern among governing boards about where the line of the foundation's involvement in institutional operations should be drawn. As foundations enlist more people of wealth and influence as members in order to enhance their fundraising capacity, and as the resources of the foundations continue to grow, it is reasonable to expect that foundation board members may seek a greater say in the institution's allocation of resources to programs—potentially coming into conflict with the prerogatives of governing boards.

Navigating all of the pressures and pitfalls described above requires careful attention to the definition of foundation-institution relationships. In 2003 AGB and CASE developed an illustrative memorandum of understanding between a foundation and its host institution or system that includes provisions related to parameters, expectations, and financial relationships. The memorandum is available on AGB's Web site. *(http:// www.agb.org/reports/2003/illustrative-memorandum-understanding-between-foundation-and-host-institution-or-system)*. Some foundations also have posted agreements with their college or university on the Internet, where they are available as useful resources for others.

FOUNDATION BOARDS: AN EVOLVING ROLE

As Joseph F. Phelan observes, "The enlightened cadre [that created the first foundation] at the University of Kansas perhaps did not itself foresee that their innovation eventually would intersect widely and nationally with the increasing popularity of state colleges and universities as objects of philanthropy. Nor might they have foreseen that the [entity] that they created [to receive] bequests and other self-motivated gifts would become—on their campus and on hundreds of others—the linchpin for earnest and determined fundraising activity."

The shift in the role of foundations from passive repositories to fundraising linchpins has been continuous, but it has accelerated in recent years. In a 2006 study conducted by CASE, 37 percent of foundations said the most common pattern was for *institutional staff* to direct and coordinate fundraising, with support from the foundation. Just three years later, in a CASE follow-up study published as a white paper, titled "Institutionally Related Foundations and the Economic Downturn," the situation had essentially reversed. The most common response (35 percent) described the foundation as almost wholly responsible for the direction and execution of fundraising.

The 2010 AGB survey produced results similar to CASE's 2009 finding: 35 percent of foundations reported that they are almost entirely responsible for the direction and execution of fundraising. At another 34 percent of foundations, institutional staff members direct fundraising with support from foundation staff and volunteers. In 17.2 percent of cases, the foundation directs and coordinates fundraising with support from institutional staff. Only 14 percent of the foundations reporting to AGB in 2010 are not engaged in fundraising and just receive, invest, and manage gifts and other assets for the institution. As such data indicate, the fundraising role of institutionally related foundations has increased significantly, with important implications for the responsibilities and functions of foundation boards.

There is extensive literature on the fundraising roles and responsibilities of board of trustees in independent colleges and universities, including a book that I wrote and AGB published in 2005 (*Securing the Future: A Fundraising Guide for Boards of Independent Colleges and Universities*). But less information has been available on the fundraising roles of boards of institutionally related foundations in the public sector. Two studies of public colleges and universities were undertaken by AGB in earlier years. In 2000, a survey of public institution campaigns was published in *A Board's Guide to Comprehensive Campaigns*, edited by Jake B. Schrum. Another study, in 2003, was published in *How Public College and University Foundation Boards Contribute to Campaign Success*, written by Royster C. Hedgepeth. But gaps in our knowledge remain, especially following a decade of rapid change.

The following chapters discuss some principles of the board's role in fundraising. They draw on previous research and writing, some of which focuses on the board role in independent colleges and universities but also has relevance to foundation boards engaged in active fundraising. They also compare current data to earlier studies of institutionally related foundations and then bring the topic up-to-date with new information from the 2010 AGB survey.

THE 2010 AGB SURVEY

The 2010 AGB survey included an online questionnaire to which 137 foundation chief executive officers responded. They mostly represented foundations serving single institutions, but a few serve multicampus systems or specific academic units within an institution. The largest number of responses was from research/doctoral universities, followed by two-year institutions, four-year master's institutions, and four-year baccalaureate institutions. Foundations represented in the survey also reflect diversity in the magnitude of their assets and private support received. The largest number of foundations (41 percent) have assets of less than $25 million, but some (11 percent) hold assets in excess of $500 million. In terms of voluntary private support, revenues range from under $1 million to more than $100 million per year.

Responses to the 2010 AGB Survey

Type of institution served by foundation	Percentage of respondents
Research/doctoral universities	38.0%
Two-year institutions	24.8%
Four-year master's institutions	22.6%
Four-year baccalaureate institutions	9.5%
Multicampus systems	2.9%
Colleges or schools with an institution	2.2%

Assets of Foundations Participating in the 2010 AGB Survey

Total of foundation assets	Percentage of survey participants
$0-25 million	41.2%
$26-50 million	7.4%
$51-150 million	22.1%
$151-500 million	18.4%
Over $500 million	11.0%

Voluntary Private Support Received By Foundations
Participating in the 2010 AGB Survey

Total private voluntary support	Percentage of survey participants
Under $1 million	17.0%
$1-5 million	38.5%
$6-10 million	11.1%
$11-25 million	12.6%
$26-50 million	6.7%
$51-100 million	5.9%
Over $100 million	8.1%

NOTE: Voluntary private support includes private gifts, grants, and bequests and excludes government support and contract revenues.

KEY FINDINGS OF THE 2010 AGB SURVEY

Findings of the 2010 AGB survey are presented and discussed in the context of the topics covered by subsequent chapters of this book. The following provides a summary of some key points:

- Institutionally related foundations vary in their roles. Some are still passive recipients of private gifts; others are evolving from a purely fiduciary role toward becoming active fundraising entities; and some are mature and sophisticated in their approach to fundraising.

- Institutionally related foundations vary widely in their size. More than 40 percent have assets of less than $25 million and only 11 percent have assets exceeding $500 million.

- Foundation chief executive officers play a central role in the leadership of most foundations and in maintaining relationships among the foundation, the institutional chief executive, and the institutional governing board. Just over one-half are also officers of their institutions.

- In the largest number of foundations, the foundation chief executive officer is primarily responsible for aligning fundraising priorities with institutional priorities and for monitoring fundraising performance.

- The most common pattern is for the foundation board to participate in cultivation, solicitation, and stewardship activities accompanied by the institution president or by development-office or foundation staff members, rather than alone.

- Foundation boards and institutional governing boards are coordinated in various ways, including overlapping membership and the efforts of institutional presidents, institutional chief advancement officers, and foundation chief executives. Some report only informal coordination or no coordination between the boards.

- Criteria applied in selecting new foundation directors include the ability to make a gift, the ability and willingness to solicit gifts, diversity considerations, and personal compatibility with other board members.
- Most foundations discuss giving expectations in the enlistment of new directors. More than one-half have a policy on board giving, but only 30 percent specify a required minimum annual gift.
- Most foundations have a standing committee on development. Most institutional governing boards do not.
- The largest number of foundation chief executives rate the foundation's development committee as "somewhat effective."
- The largest number of foundation chief executives rate the foundation board as "somewhat effective" in fundraising activities such as identifying new prospects and participating in cultivation, solicitation, and stewardship.
- About 55 percent of foundations are in the public phase of a campaign or have recently completed a campaign.
- Average campaign goals range from over $400 million at research/doctoral institutions to about $9 million at two-year institutions.
- The institution chief executive (president/chancellor) has the strongest influence in establishing the goals and objectives of campaigns.
- The institution's chief executive, foundation board members, the foundation CEO, and the institution's chief advancement officer are the primary solicitors of gifts to a campaign's nucleus fund (during the quiet phase).
- Most institutions create a special campaign leadership committee for a campaign, including members of the foundation board, members of the institution's governing board, and others.

CASE STUDY

RESTRUCTURING THE FOUNDATION BOARD FOR ENHANCED PERFORMANCE:
INDIANA UNIVERSITY FOUNDATON

Created in 1936, the Indiana University Foundation receives some $150 million annually in gifts and, at $1.5 billion, manages one of the nation's largest public university endowments. Eugene R. Tempel was appointed president of the foundation in 2008, after serving for 11 years as executive director of the Center for Philanthropy at Indiana University. He is the university's chief advancement officer and holds appointments as professor of philanthropic studies and of higher education.

Like all institutionally related foundations, IUF faced the need to ensure the board's accountability in governance and fiduciary matters while also enhancing board members' engagement in fundraising. Although individually generous, directors had been primarily focused on the board's fiduciary responsibilities, with less emphasis on fundraising. Research indicated that smaller boards could be more effective in governing, and some directors periodically raised the issue of the number of directors—nearly 70 principal and life directors—all of whom had legal responsibility for actions of the board. Finally, the presidents of the foundation and the university—who is also chair of the foundation board—and others saw the great potential of these leaders as fundraisers.

Conversations that took place during two years of board meetings, board retreats, and individual interactions led to a restructuring of the board. It was, Tempel notes, a sensitive process that required careful attention to individuals' feelings and perceptions.

The bylaws were revised to create two categories of directors within one board. The board now includes up to 100 members who serve three-year terms and can be re-elected to additional terms without limit. Within the larger board is a smaller group, which Tempel calls the "fiduciary directors," who have legal responsibilities typical of most nonprofit board directors, such as investments, finance and budget, audit, real estate, legal issues, and the like. This subset of the board includes up to 24 members who are limited to four three-year terms, after which they may continue to serve on the larger board. The bylaws, revised with the assistance of legal counsel, carefully distinguish between the responsibilities of those with and without fiduciary responsibilities. In both the old and new structures, university officers serve as consulting members to committees of the board.

The restructuring has strengthened the foundation's accountability and made it possible to enhance the board's fundraising role. Director orientation now directly addresses fundraising as well as legal responsibilities. The board has established four new fundraising committees, each related to one of the university's overarching academic priorities. Board members are also more focused on fundraising efforts for campuses, schools, academic units, and programs. All directors are asked to make annual gifts of $10,000 or more and to consider major and planned gifts. Most participate at these levels, although it is not a formal requirement.

Asked for his advice on undertaking such a restructuring, Tempel said: "Move deliberately, but carefully. You need to make judgments about which skills are best suited to fiduciary and other roles on the board, but you also want to avoid any perception that non-fiduciary members of the larger board are second-class citizens. They are not, because their fundraising responsibilities are equally important."

CHAPTER 2

AN OVERVIEW OF FUNDRAISING FOR HIGHER EDUCATION

This chapter provides a general overview of higher education fundraising, including the way in which advancement or development offices are organized and staffed, the various programs that are included in a comprehensive development program, and some fundamental fundraising principles. The discussion is intended to provide an introduction to the field for those who may be relatively new to their roles as foundation board members. Those who are experienced and knowledgeable may prefer to skip this chapter and go directly to Chapter 3, although some may find this chapter useful as a refresher.

Higher education fundraising differs in many ways from that of other nonprofit organizations with which foundation board members may be familiar through their other volunteer activities. For example, colleges and universities have a built-in (if relatively finite) constituency of alumni. This provides an advantage over nonprofit organizations that must rely on such techniques as fundraising events or rented mailing lists to identify potential donors. At the same time, colleges and universities may present less compelling causes than some nonprofits, because their missions lack the urgency of many human-service organizations. That means that higher education institutions usually focus their fundraising efforts on people who have some natural linkage—for example, alumni, parents, and others who have had some personal engagement with the institution.

Such realities call for an approach to fundraising that places a high value on developing and maintaining relationships with donors over the long term. Most alumni will not reach their peak giving years until decades after graduation, so colleges and universities need to make an ongoing investment in relationships with them before significant financial returns can be realized. For the same reason, institutions must be cautious about employing the more aggressive, short-term techniques used by some nonprofits and political campaigns. That is not to suggest that fundraising in higher education is less purposeful or goal-driven than in other organizations, but rather that volunteer leaders, including members of the foundation board, need to understand the style as well as the methods of fundraising appropriate to higher education's unique environment. Comparison with different types of organizations may not be valid.

TAKEAWAYS FOR FOUNDATION BOARD MEMBERS

- In order to work as effective partners with the campus leader and fundraising staff, and to monitor and support the development program, foundation directors need a fundamental knowledge of fundraising principles.

- Some key components of a fundraising program are: annual giving, major gifts, planned gifts, corporate and foundation support, advancement services, and alumni relations programs.

- Foundation board members need not be intimately familiar with the operations of the foundation staff or development office at their particular institutions, but they should understand the basic organizational model.

- While there is no "right" model for organizing fundraising, the approach a particular institution takes should be compatible with its overall organization, tradition, and culture.

- Board members should be assured that a system for managing relationships with donor prospects is in place and should respect the need for coordination with the overall operation in conducting their own fundraising activities.

It is also important to consider carefully the relevance of successful fundraising strategies drawn from other colleges and universities that have different histories, constituencies, and traditions. Obviously, the University of California, Berkeley, and the University of California, Los Angeles are not likely to be good models for a community college with a young alumni body. A young urban institution may need to take an approach that is quite different from a large state university with a strong tradition of intercollegiate athletics. Even two public institutions that appear to be alike in some respects, perhaps of the same age and with a similar array of academic programs, may be quite different from a fundraising perspective. For example, a residential campus in a small town or rural setting may engender closer bonds with its alumni than an urban campus that enrolls many part-time students. It is important for foundation board members to understand and acknowledge these differences, so as to establish realistic expectations for the institution's leadership as well as for themselves. Appropriate comparisons with other institutions may provide a guide to what fundraising efforts may work and what may be appropriate goals, but it is important that the selection of peers be based on relevant variables.

Foundation board members do not need to be experts on the technical points of fundraising in order to meet their responsibilities. But to work as effective partners with the president or chancellor and advancement or foundation staff, and to monitor and support the overall development program, they do need a basic understanding of fundraising principles and the organization and management of the typical development program. This chapter provides a quick overview of the elements of a typical college or university fundraising program and operation.

SOME ESSENTIAL VOCABULARY

The vocabulary used to describe fundraising and related functions in higher education institutions sometimes can be confusing, and it is continuously evolving. Since the Council for Advancement and Support of Education (CASE) was founded in 1974, the concept of "institutional advancement," or just "advancement," has gained wide acceptance on campuses. Advancement is an umbrella term encompassing the activities of alumni relations, communications/marketing, and fundraising or development. These were once separate and somewhat disconnected campus functions, but the need for coordination and integration is now generally recognized—although not always achieved or reflected in organizational structures.

The term "development" originated in the early part of the 20th century and originally meant something similar to what "advancement" means today: a long-term, comprehensive program for growing and strengthening the institution. Over the years, the term became synonymous with fundraising. Today, many campuses have an "advancement office," which may or may not encompass all three fields, though many still call the office responsible for fundraising the "development office." Many institutions have a senior officer designated as "vice president for advancement," which implies responsibility for all three advancement functions. Others use such titles as "vice president for development and alumni relations," "vice president for university relations and development," or "vice president for external affairs." But the span of the individual's actual responsibilities may not always be evident from the title.

Some larger institutions, both private and public, have divided advancement responsibilities between two vice presidents, one managing development and alumni relations programs and another responsible for communications and marketing. This model is sometimes adopted because communications and marketing have become substantial enterprises that are central to student recruitment and/or government relations. Where communications and marketing are managed by an individual different from the manager of fundraising, the development office often has a smaller internal unit with focused responsibility for development communications.

The situation at public institutions is often even more complicated. If fundraising is managed by a foundation, under the direction of an executive director or president who is not also a campus officer, and a different campus officer holds responsibility for communications and alumni relations, then the institutional-advancement model does not technically exist, even if the term may be part of the title of an individual or office.

This book uses the terms "fundraising" and "development" interchangeably. It generally refers to the senior campus officer responsible for fundraising as the "chief advancement officer," without regard to whether the individual actually holds the wider span of responsibility implied by the advancement term. It refers to the chief executive officer of the foundation, who may be titled "executive director," "president," or something else, simply as the "foundation CEO" or the "foundation chief executive." The fundraising roles of advancement officers, presidents, and boards are discussed further in Chapter 3. In that context, and in others in this book, the term "chief advancement officer" is used generically to mean the development or advancement professional who works with the board and institution chief executive on fundraising. To keep things as simple as possible in the balance of this book, the chief advancement officer and the foundation CEO generally are distinguished only where the division of responsibilities between those positions is relevant to the discussion.

As discussed in Chapter 1, responses to the 2010 AGB survey revealed that most foundation executives (52 percent) are also officers of their institutions, while 48 percent are not. It should be noted that in a study conducted by AGB and CASE in the late 1990s (reported in *College and University Foundations*, published by AGB in 1997), 65 percent of foundation chief executives also served as their institution's chief advancement officer. The difference between that survey and the 2010 AGB survey may reflect a trend toward more-independent foundations with chief executives who report only to the foundation board.

Even at small colleges, the advancement staff is likely to possess significant professional experience and expertise. At major universities, the fundraising staff includes dozens or even hundreds of professionals, many with highly specialized skills. Development professionals acquire their professional training primarily through conferences, institutes, and workshops offered by CASE and other professional organizations, although a growing number of commercial firms and consultants offer training programs. The professional culture of development includes mentoring and communication among colleagues across institutions. Information about successful strategies, but not individual donors, is readily shared.

Higher education advancement once was a profession that people entered through an indirect route. Some development officers moved into higher education from the business world or another field, and others had a background on the faculty. Today, advancement has become a recognized profession, and it is not uncommon to meet students who are preparing for a career in the field. In recent years, formal academic courses in advancement and fundraising also have emerged as part of the curriculum at many colleges and universities. They are sometimes offered through schools of professional studies, or as part of a broader program in nonprofit management.

In the vibrant economy of the mid-2000s, the demand for fundraising professionals, especially major gift officers, exceeded the pool of people with experience. A number of institutions established programs to recruit gift officers from other professions and provide them with fundraising training. The fundraising job market cooled during the recession that began in 2007, but from the perspective of 2011, there appear again to be numerous opportunities for people who are interested in a career in higher education advancement.

ORGANIZATION AND MANAGEMENT OF FUNDRAISING

Foundation board members need not be intimately familiar with the operations of the foundation staff or institutional development office that supports them. Indeed, too much familiarity may lead to inappropriate involvement in administration of the foundation, college, or university. But foundation directors or trustees should at least understand the basic organizational model that is practiced at their institution.

One fundamental distinction is whether fundraising staff are employed by the foundation or the institution. At some institutions, fundraising staff are exclusively employees of the foundation. At others, they are employed by the institution. In some cases, institutional employees serve the foundation, but the foundation compensates the institution for the portion of time these employees devote to foundation business. (This is related to the discussion in Chapter 1 regarding dependent, interdependent, and independent foundations.) Regardless of the specific arrangements, the array of skills and specialties represented on the fundraising professional staff will be much the same from one institution to another, even at private and public institutions. That is because fundraising has become professionalized and specialized, and requires people with the same skills regardless of their employer's legal status—just as a similar array of medical specialists would be found at public and nonprofit hospitals.

As explained above, many small colleges follow the institutional-advancement model, with a vice president for advancement responsible for the areas of alumni relations, communications/marketing, and fundraising or development. In some large universities, advancement responsibilities may be divided between vice presidents for development and for communications and marketing.

Another major consideration in the organization of development staff, especially at large universities, is the question of centralization and decentralization. In addition to the institution's central development office or the foundation office, individual colleges, schools, centers, institutes, and other units within the university often employ development staff—ranging from a single individual to large enterprises—based in the unit and working closely with the dean or director. Generally three models of organization are common in this situation. In a centralized system, all development staff report ultimately to the chief advancement officer, possibly with assignments to pursue gifts for particular units' objectives. Other universities have decentralized systems, in which unit-based staff report to and are compensated by the dean or director, with little or no relationship to the vice president or central development office. The third approach is called the "hybrid model," in which unit-based staff members have dual reporting relationships: one to the unit executive (such as a dean) and another to the vice president for development or advancement. Financial support for unit-based positions is often shared between the unit and the central office or foundation budget under such a model.

There is no "right" model among these three, and the approach that a particular institution takes should be compatible with its overall organization, tradition, and culture. Trying to impose a highly centralized fundraising model on a decentralized university may produce more problems and controversies than efficiencies. At the same time, a totally decentralized model can cause destructive competition and redundancy. Foundation directors should not encourage a particular model for their institution just because they may have seen it succeed elsewhere, but they should ask about the rationale for the structure that exists.

What is important under any of these models is that a system for managing relationships with prospects is in place and enforced in order to avoid internal competition for access to them and the appearance of disarray in communications with donors. Board members should be assured that such a system is in place and should respect the need for coordination with the overall operation in conducting their own fundraising activities.

COMPONENTS OF A FUNDRAISING PROGRAM

While some see the term "fundraising" as synonymous with just asking for money, the development program on most campuses includes several distinct activities that employ different techniques, target different constituencies, and produce gifts useful for different purposes. These components will be in place whether fundraising is the responsibility of the institution, the foundation, or some mix. Although college and university fundraising is an ongoing effort, some of the most effective results are achieved during formal campaigns. What follows here are the permanent components one would expect to find in a typical fundraising operation.

Annual Giving

The annual giving program (or the annual fund) is the foundation of the fundraising effort. It raises relatively modest but recurring gifts in support of the institution's operating budget from a broad base of donors, including alumni, parents, and others. Some colleges and universities define the annual fund to encompass only unrestricted gifts; others may also include gifts that support current operations but are designated to specific programs or academic units. Another way of defining the annual fund is to set a dollar limit—for example, counting any gift for current operating support that is less than $10,000 as part of the annual fund—and considering anything larger to be a major gift.

Because they appeal to broad audiences, annual giving programs rely substantially on direct-mail, phone solicitations and, increasingly, the Internet. Some institutions still use organized volunteers for phone solicitations (the traditional "phonathon"), but large universities with lists of tens or hundreds of thousands of alumni to call use paid student callers or commercial telemarketing firms. While use of the Internet in soliciting annual fund gifts is growing, it has yet to replace the more traditional tools of mail and phone, especially in reaching older alumni and donors. Research suggests that there is a clear generational divide, with older donors preferring to make gifts through mail and younger donors more responsive to Internet-based communications. The use of text messaging, which proved successful in the 2008 presidential campaign and in fundraising by the Red Cross following the 2010 Haitian earthquake, is not widely used in fundraising for higher education, although some institutions are experimenting with it. The annual fund techniques applied by a specific college or university should be a good fit with the demographics of its constituency. But even institutions with many older alumni need to be developing a strong presence online, including on social-networking sites, since the future clearly will bring increased importance of these tools.

Personal solicitation of annual fund gifts is important at higher levels of giving. Some institutions—for example, private colleges with a tradition of having class agents—use volunteers in this role. Members of the foundation board may be personally solicited for annual gifts by the board chair or chair of the development committee. Large development offices employ staff members who solicit annual fund gifts on a full-time basis. These individuals are sometimes called "road warriors" because they constantly travel. Such positions often are considered entry-level and engage young development professionals who advance to larger gift solicitations after a few years in the trenches of the annual fund.

For some colleges and universities, annual giving is an important source of revenue. For others, including most public institutions, the annual fund provides only a small portion of the total operating budget. But even in such instances, it is an essential component of a comprehensive, long-term development effort. Conventional wisdom, supported by recent research, tells us that the annual giving program helps develop a habit of giving among donors and provides them the opportunity to self-identify as prospects for major gifts. Some follow the strategy of "minus 2, plus 3," believing that it is important to secure gifts from students in their last two undergraduate years and in the three years immediately following their graduation, in order to establish a pattern of giving that may continue for their lifetimes.

The annual giving program also generates the alumni participation rate, which is defined as the percentage of alumni who make some gift in a given year. The participation rate has gained considerable attention, in part because *U.S. News & World Report* uses the rate as a part of the formula by which it ranks colleges and universities. Thus, many institutions, including those for which the annual fund is an inconsequential portion of total revenues, have invested in strengthening their annual giving programs. Some are even willing to reduce the cost-effectiveness of the program in the short run to gain the long-term benefits of a base of regular donors and potentially higher *U.S. News* rankings. *U.S. News* regards the alumni participation rate as an indicator of graduates' satisfaction with their educational experience, although that assumption is easily challenged.

Because many annual fund programs are staff-driven, foundation directors may find that they have little role in this area of fundraising beyond ensuring their own unanimous participation in annual giving. Nonetheless, boards should monitor the performance of the annual giving program from year to year. That requires the board to understand how the annual fund is defined at their foundation or institution and to ensure that common metrics are used in comparisons with benchmark institutions. Data compiled in the annual *Voluntary Support of Education* survey by the Council for Aid to Education (CAE) show gifts in support of current operations in the categories of "unrestricted" and "restricted," but some college and university annual funds may include gifts from both categories. If restricted gifts are included in the annual fund, it is important to distinguish those that are what David Dunlop, a long-serving former development professional at Cornell University and a prolific writer and speaker in the field, calls "regular gifts"— likely to be repeated by the donor every year—from those that may reflect one-time gifts (or grants) in support of a special project or program. It also is important to remember that unrestricted bequests will be accounted for as unrestricted operating revenue, although they generally should be ignored when evaluating the annual giving program or projecting the revenues it may produce.

In evaluating the annual fund program, board members should be realistic in terms of current trends. These include the rise of a new generation of donors who are disinclined to make unrestricted gifts, preferring at a minimum to restrict their gifts to a specific program or purpose of the college or university—for example, the library or undergraduate scholarships. In addition, while some institutions have succeeded in increasing their alumni participation rate, alumni participation on a national basis has remained flat or declined. As discussed in Chapter 1, alumni participation at public institutions generally lags behind that at private colleges and universities primarily as a result of the publics' larger, more diverse alumni bodies.

Some observers have expressed concern that alumni participation may be more difficult to increase or even sustain in the future. The thinking is that more students are graduating with higher levels of debt and many young, first-time donors appear to be attracted to organizations working to support social causes rather than colleges and universities. In addition, some graduates today may hold a different mindset about their educational experience. Whereas earlier generations viewed a college education as a privilege and felt compelled to repay for the opportunity, the expansion of higher education may result in more graduates who see it as a right and may feel little obligation to continue supporting their colleges and universities in appreciation for the services they received there. And, of course, rising tuitions have resulted in higher levels of student-loan debt, which also may inhibit giving in the early years following graduation, when student-loan repayments may consume a significant portion of income. In sum, current and future graduates may feel less gratitude or obligation to give back. This situation presents a challenge and will require that institutions invest even more in building community among their students and alumni and in making the case for why alumni annual support is important.

Major Gifts

Because they are defined by a dollar amount, major gifts vary from one campus to another, depending on the fundraising history and capacity of each institution. A commonly applied standard considers a five-year commitment of $50,000 ($10,000 per year for five years) to be a major gift and anything less than $10,000 on an annual basis to be part of annual giving. But some institutions will define a major gift as $100,000 or more, assuming a five-year payment schedule.

Major gifts generally are restricted; that is, the donor will identify a specific purpose or program rather than leaving the use of the gift to the discretion of the foundation or institution. The donor may wish to support a current program, capital project, or the endowment. Few major gifts are completely unrestricted, except for bequests, which sometimes name the foundation or institution as the recipient without any further designation.

During the 1990s, the term "principal gifts" came into use in higher education fundraising. Principal gifts are large major gifts that have a transformational impact on the institution and are among the largest gifts the institution ever will receive. Many headline-attracting gifts—those in the tens or hundreds of millions of dollars that prompt the establishment of new research centers or the renaming of entire institutions—provide examples of principal gifts. Again, the definition is related to a dollar amount and varies among institutions. Larger universities have established a specialized unit of major gifts staff to manage relationships with principal gift prospects and donors. And some have expanded the definition to encompass those donors who are among the most important to the institution or with whom the president or chancellor needs to be most closely engaged, regardless of whether their gift capacity meets some arbitrary level.

The Five I's

The fundraising literature describes a process in the development of major gift donors that requires a consistent and patient approach. G.T. "Buck" Smith, a former development officer who is now president of Davis and Elkins College in West Virginia, has described the stages of an individual's growing relationship with an institution. His formulation is known as the "five I's." The relationship starts with interest, which is followed by gaining information, which leads to involvement, which helps to build the person's identity with the institution, leading eventually to investment in the form of giving. The cultivation of a major gift prospect is intended to move him or her along this continuum. An initiative undertaken to produce such movement is known to development professionals as a "move," and the systematic pursuit of such initiatives is called "moves management"—terms introduced to the field by David Dunlop, a writer and former senior development officer at Cornell University.

One basic concept is depicted by the fundraising pyramid. Shown in Figure 2.1, the pyramid illustrates how the fundraising program is built on the institution's natural constituency at the base. This constituency generally includes every individual or organization with whom the institution has had any connection—usually alumni, parents, friends, past donors, former patients of a university medical center, and other groups.

Figure 2.1
The Fundraising Pyramid

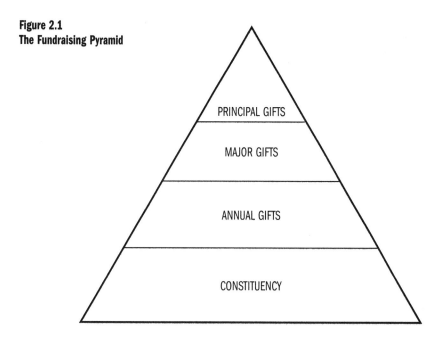

Fundraising consultant Henry A. Rosso, in the 1991 edition of his book *Achieving Excellence in Fundraising* (Jossey-Bass), explained that only some constituents are actually prospects for fundraising: those who have linkage to the institution (for example, as a parent or alumnus), the ability to make a gift (that is, financial capacity), and interest in the institution's well-being. According to Rosso, unless a person meets all three criteria, he or she is not highly likely to be a prospect for giving to the college or university.

Public colleges and universities may find it more possible than do independent institutions to attract the interest of people who do not have a formal affiliation (for example, as an alumnus), because they can make the case that their programs benefit the economy of the entire community or state and therefore are important to all citizens. This argument certainly can be persuasive with corporations and foundations that have a principal interest in the state or region. In earlier decades, it was not unusual to find people who had been successful in business and who were not graduates of a college or university. A university serving their state or community might be able to develop their interest and a sense of affiliation similar to that of a graduate.

Although I have seen no research to support the point, I suspect that this may be more difficult today, when most successful people have some relationship with a college or university, either by virtue of having attended themselves or through their families. Rosso's emphasis on the confluence of linkage, ability, and interest may be even more applicable. And, of course, it must be remembered, the three characteristics do not always coincide. To use the old expression, "if I had a nickel" for every time a graduate of one of the institutions I served as a development officer—including some individuals with substantial capacity—told me that he or she had no interest in making a gift, I would qualify as a major prospect myself! Linkage does not guarantee interest, but it is usually a good starting point for dialogue that may increase it over time.

Some prospects will become donors to the annual fund. Some may develop sufficient interest (and have sufficient capacity) to become major gift donors. A few may, over a long period of cultivation, join the few who make the principal gifts that transform the institution. As the pyramid shape suggests, the number of individuals in each category declines as one moves toward the apex. However, a pyramid depicting revenues from each group might be inverted, reflecting the fact that major and principal gifts account for a much larger portion of total giving than do the many smaller gifts in the annual fund.

Dunlop argues that the small number of the institution's donors capable of making principal gifts should be the focus of what he calls "nurturing fundraising." In this approach, the emphasis is on building and maintaining the relationship between the individual and the institution, rather than the actual solicitation of gifts. The goal is to strengthen the relationship to the point where a person becomes so deeply identified with and committed to the institution that his or her desire to make a significant investment in its work requires relatively little prompting. This style of fundraising is a long-term process, perhaps extending over the individual's lifetime. As Dunlop emphasizes, this approach does not preclude the aggressive techniques of the annual fund or capital campaign, but it should be adopted for a few of the institution's most dedicated and promising gift prospects.

As the five I's and the fundraising pyramid suggest, major gift fundraising is a process that requires time and consistent attention. (The process is described and depicted in Chapter 5 of this book, which describes the engagement of foundation directors in each stage.) As in courtship, a period of dating generally is required before a proposal will be seriously considered, and the process cannot be accelerated simply because one of the parties may feel impatient. Foundation directors should recognize that if an institution has not been engaged in the systematic identification and cultivation of potential major gift donors on a continuous basis, it may be ill-prepared to solicit major gifts. While there may be some surprises, most major donors will have demonstrated their dedication to the institution for a long time before they commit to a major or principal gift.

I have known some board members who make a comparison between major gift fundraising and commercial or financial sales, believing that merely increasing the effort or hiring more aggressive and persuasive gift officers will quickly produce an increase in major gifts. There is, indeed, a relationship between effort and results, but the nature of giving is quite different from that of commercial transactions. While the latter, by definition, involves a quid pro quo in which the buyer gains some advantage, giving is by definition an emotionally based decision. The ability of an individual development officer, or even an institution's president, to influence the motivations of a prospect may be limited. The process usually requires developing a relationship over time and, in many cases, waiting patiently until the donor's circumstances produce a moment when he or she is prepared to make the gift.

During the booms of the late 1990s and mid-2000s, some observers argued that the traditional approach implied by the five I's and the fundraising pyramid was an obsolete concept. They cited the rise of entrepreneurial donors, who are driven by their own priorities and interests rather than traditional institutional loyalties. Such philanthropists evaluate giving opportunities as they do their investments, providing support to organizations they deem to be best able to help fulfill their own philanthropic objectives. Some argue that cultivating relationships with such donors is less important than developing exciting ideas and demonstrating responsiveness to their interests.

If correct, this situation presents an even more challenging fundraising environment for public colleges and universities. As discussed above, many institutions now need more unrestricted gifts to support current operating budgets. That need faces the disinclination of entrepreneurial donors to give to established programs or to activities in which they have little personal involvement. The new ideas that such donors may bring to the discussion are less attractive to institutions working to maintain sufficient revenue to support essential programs.

Some colleges and universities have developed approaches to engaging entrepreneurial donors and some successes have been reported. In an article in the February 2006 issue of the *International Journal of Educational Advancement*, "When Venture Philanthropy Rocks the Ivory Tower," Luisa Boverini tells the story of venture philanthropist Jane Brown, who lives in Baltimore, and her involvement with her alma mater, the University of Maryland at College Park. As a member of its foundation board, Brown has worked with the university to develop its Baltimore Incentive Awards, a scholarship program that supports students from nine city high schools who attend Maryland. She is a volunteer in the J-Lab, a program of the university's School of Journalism, and at an interdisciplinary center called the Democracy Collaborative, which studies economic development in poor communities. These programs are consistent with her interest in reducing poverty in her home city and with her desire for active involvement in the programs she supports. The case provides an example of how a university with an array of programs and initiatives can connect a donor whose priority may be the social impact of a higher education institution rather than the mission of higher education per se.

Whether entrepreneurial donors will really prove so different over the longer run is worthy of consideration. There clearly is a new attitude among young donors, especially those who accumulated their wealth as entrepreneurs. They prefer to designate their gifts for specific purposes and demand accountability for accomplishing those purposes. However, donors are still more inclined to give when and where they are involved, and significant gifts flow from a relationship rather than just by asking for money. Those are traditional ideas that are not inconsistent with the behavior of younger donors. And it may be that donors who are entrepreneurial today will look to institutions like colleges and universities to secure their legacies once they reach later stages of their lives.

To be sure, the ability of colleges and universities to secure totally unrestricted gifts is made more challenging by the perspectives of entrepreneurial philanthropists. That means institutions will need to be clear about their need for support and the relevance of their missions. Demands for accountability and transparency are not likely to abate, and many donors will insist on having a voice in how their gifts are applied. That will challenge colleges and universities to accommodate the attitudes of a new generation of donors, but it is not likely to invalidate proven fundraising strategies.

Foundation directors should bear in mind that an institution's fundraising potential is determined largely by the number and financial capacity of its natural prospects. Most development offices have a database of major gift prospects who have been rated in terms of their estimated financial capacity and other variables. Effective cultivation efforts can raise the interest and commitment of prospective donors so that their gifts approach their financial capacity to give. In addition, prospect research may uncover among the institution's natural constituency new prospects with previously unrecognized wealth.

Regardless, the estimated giving capacity of the institution's constituency (assuming that the information on it is accurate) defines the realistic limits of what the college or university is likely to achieve in its fundraising efforts. Goals need to be set reflecting that reality. It is not useful for board members and others to engage in wishful thinking about fundraising. Any hopes that substantial funds can be raised from strangers with no relationship to the institution or that unexpected windfalls will enable a college or university to achieve ambitious goals without the sacrificial giving of its own board leaders and other insiders are generally illusions.

As in annual giving programs, there has been a trend since the 1990s toward increasingly staff-driven major gift programs, particularly at large universities. On many campuses, major gift development officers actively cultivate and solicit major gift donor prospects and are among the best-compensated members of the development staff. Major gift officers may accompany the president, a dean, a board member, or another volunteer leader on visits to prospects, but some also interact with major prospects alone. In part, the growing importance of planned giving has fostered this increased role for professional staff. Many major gifts now include some element of planned giving, which is discussed later in this chapter.

Despite the increase in staff-driven major gift programs, the leadership and partici-pation of board members and other volunteers in identifying, cultivating, and soliciting major and principal gift donors is still crucial, for various important reasons. Chapter 3 of this book discusses the fundraising partnership and the important role that foundation directors can play in the major gifts process.

The increased role of major gift officers has led to more-structured management of the major gifts process. The planning and monitoring of systematic interactions with major gift prospects, similar to a sales-management system in businesses, is practiced in nearly all well-run development offices. Major gift officers usually have well-defined performance goals, and some institutions offer financial incentives to major gifts staff. The subject of incentive-based compensation is still controversial in higher education fundraising. Most institutions that offer incentives base them not only on dollars raised, but also on measurable activity goals, such as the number of new prospects identified and the number of cultivation and solicitation visits completed.

Some foundation directors who are familiar with compensation plans in business may favor the idea of compensating development officers based on the revenues they produce, perhaps even paying them a percentage of the revenue they generate. But the payment of commissions is almost universally considered unethical in fundraising and is prohibited under the ethical codes of CASE and other leading professional organiza-tions in the field. Even tying compensation less directly to funds raised is a complicated and controversial matter. This is true in part because creating incentives for major gift officers to take quick action risks harming the institution's long-term relationships with donors. It is also possible that a fundraiser's self-interest in a gift, if known to the pro-spective donor, might undermine the trust essential to the philanthropic relationship. In addition, the development officer often is but one of many individuals who participate in obtaining a gift. For example, the relationship of the president or a foundation board member may be the most important determinant in a donor's decision to give. It may not be possible to attribute the gift to any one member of the team, and it is important not to establish incentives that might undermine a team approach.

Again, it is important to keep in mind the critical distinction between sales of products or services in the for-profit sector and the solicitation of philanthropic gifts. The former are almost always related to the self-interest and needs of the customer. Philanthropic gifts always involve an important element of altruism and often reflect the donor's emotional bonds with an institution and the people associated with its leadership. Although sales and fundraising have some operational principles in common, they are two very different types of transactions and require different approaches.

Planned Gifts

Planned gifts involve some aspect of financial and estate planning. The simplest form of planned gift is a bequest, which is a provision in the individual's will or revocable trust providing for a gift to the institution upon the donor's death. Other common planned giving arrangements, such as charitable remainder trusts and charitable gift annuities, provide for a lifetime income to the donor or another beneficiary. Under most planned giving arrangements, the funds are not fully available for use by the institution until the death of the donor or other income beneficiary. Thus, it is important to account for planned gift commitments differently from outright gifts or short-term pledges and to be cognizant of the difference in the foundation's and institution's financial planning.

An increasing number of major gifts involve at least some element of planned giving, and the percentage of major gifts that take this approach is increasing. This is true in part because many people hold appreciated assets and are attracted by the favorable treatment of capital gains offered by some forms of planned giving. It also may reflect the growing financial sophistication of many donors and their desire to retain some control over assets or to receive lifetime income from charitable trusts or annuities in light of economic uncertainty. And, of course, it reflects the general aging of the population, with older donors both holding greater wealth and being more inclined to think about the disposition of their estates.

Planned gifts may be irrevocably committed by the donor today, but they generally are not available to the institution or foundation for many years. Given that the timing of their receipt is uncertain, they generally should not be budgeted toward current operations or be relied upon to defray the cost of new facilities. Perhaps the most practical use of planned gifts is in building the foundation's endowment.

Because planned giving officers possess specialized expertise, they are in particularly high demand, and their salaries have risen over the past decade. Some prefer to be known as "gift planners," viewing their role as serving both the institution and the donor by developing plans that meets the institution's needs and the donor's financial goals and circumstances.

Corporate and Foundation Support

A typical development office or foundation staff includes professionals experienced in raising money from corporations and private foundations. In small shops, these responsibilities often are combined in the job of one person, while larger operations may have separate staffs in each area. These individuals often work with faculty members to develop proposals responsive to the guidelines of grantors and consistent with the institution's academic strengths and goals. Recognizing the close link between academic priorities and corporate and foundation interests, some research universities have created professional staff positions that report jointly to the development office and an academic officer, such as the provost. In universities with significant research enterprises, the line sometimes may be blurred between what is considered foundation or corporate philanthropy and what is a contractual relationship; the latter often is managed through a separate office of sponsored research or a research foundation.

Directors of institutionally related foundations can be helpful in raising funds from companies or private foundations with which they have some relationship. But with larger corporations and private foundations, grantmaking has become increasingly professionalized. The process often follows clear policies and priorities and results from the analysis and recommendations of professional staff rather than the personal interests of foundation trustees or corporate directors. In that environment, support for a college or university is based not so much on its needs as on its capabilities to carry out the philanthropic goals of the company or the foundation. The board of an institutionally related foundation may be able to help open the door to such funders, but in most cases, the institution will need to compete on the merits of its own capacity to deliver programs that further the grantmaker's philanthropic priorities. Small family foundations are the exception. When the foundation is controlled by an individual or members of a family, its grants reflect the personal interests of those individuals. Raising funds from a family foundation is thus more like raising funds from an individual donor than from a professionally managed private foundation.

Advancement Services

One of the most rapidly growing components of modern development offices includes the back-office functions of prospect research, gift accounting, alumni records, information-systems management, data analysis, and related activities. These are known collectively as advancement services. Volunteer leaders may rarely interact with the advancement-services staff directly, but they will be the recipients of its products in the form of reports, research profiles, and other information.

The area of prospect research has grown rapidly and become professionalized. Development staff members who work in this field are highly sophisticated in their methods and have their own national professional association. A competitive environment in fundraising has created a need for more-extensive and relevant information. Commercially available electronic databases that include the interests and financial resources of prospective donors and the vast resources of the Web have enabled prospect researchers to meet that need. Once reactive in their approach, providing information on individuals in response to requests from development officers, most prospect research offices are now proactive, working hand-in-hand with development officers in identifying prospects with the capacity for major gifts.

Colleges and universities also have become increasingly sophisticated in their capacity for data mining and predictive modeling, applying the techniques and tools of commercial marketers. Often with the assistance of commercial firms, development offices analyze previous giving histories and the demographics of their constituencies to identify patterns that can drive the allocation of fundraising resources, in order to gain the maximum impact with increased efficiency.

An area of growing emphasis in well-managed development offices is known as donor relations or stewardship. Because past donors are the best prospects for future gifts and because most colleges and universities do not raise significant funds from beyond their own constituencies, it is vital to maintain the flow of communication and to tend carefully to the relationship with previous donors. This includes recognizing donors, providing donors with regular reports concerning the impact of their gifts, and other activities intended to keep those individuals engaged with and informed about the institution.

Stewardship always has been an important aspect of fundraising, but in the past decade, it has become more systematic as development-office staff positions have been created to manage the overall process. Those positions may be a part of the advancement services area or located in a different place on the development office's organizational chart, depending on the philosophy and resources of the particular institution and its chief advancement officer.

Alumni Relations Programs

In many colleges and universities, the alumni-relations office does not have direct responsibility for fundraising. Its mission, generally, is to build the loyalty and commitment of alumni by providing services and managing events and activities that help build bonds and keep alumni informed. Some like to describe the distinction between alumni relations and development as "friend raising" versus "fundraising." The alumni relations office may be a part of the college or university, or alumni relations programs may be managed by the foundation. Like institutionally related foundations, alumni associations have a range of relationships with their institutions, from dependence to interdependence to independence.

In the early years of organized fundraising in American colleges and universities, alumni associations took the lead in creating alumni funds to receive the regular gifts of graduates, with fundraising often related to class reunions or other alumni activities. But the trend of recent decades has been for the institution's development office or a foundation to manage the annual fund as part of an integrated fundraising program.

There are different professional cultures within institutional advancement. Alumni-relations staff and development staff often have somewhat different perspectives and priorities. That may be especially true if the alumni relations office is part of the institution and fundraising staff are employed by the foundation.

Development staff members often are focused on the small proportion of alumni who have the capacity to make major gifts. Those officials would prefer to see most of the attention and resources of the institution directed in support of building relationships with such prospective donors. Alumni-relations staff members work with a broader constituency of all alumni to involve them in activities beyond fundraising—including, for example, assisting in the recruitment of new students and communicating with the state legislature about higher education appropriations. Such different perspectives are understandable, given the different responsibilities of alumni relations and development offices, and they may indeed help keep the two in a healthy balance. (The relationship may be analogous to that between the sales and marketing staffs of businesses.)

In sum, institutional advancement today is a highly organized and professional activity at most colleges and universities. As described in Chapter 3, members of the foundation board are part of a fundraising team that includes the institution's president or chancellor and development officers with specialized and considerable skills. Teamwork between the board and the staff does not require that foundation directors learn all of the professional jargon of development or become experts in particular methods. But the board's general understanding of the development-office operation and professional principles is essential to making the partnership work effectively.

Questions for Foundation Boards to Consider

- Do foundation directors understand how fundraising in higher education differs from fundraising elsewhere?

- Are foundation directors conversant with the distinctions between such terms as annual giving, major gifts, and planned gifts, as well as the place of each in building the foundation's financial resources?

- Do foundation directors understand the unique history, culture, and characteristics of the institution they serve and acknowledge that strategies that may have worked well in very different settings may not be transferrable?

- Do foundation directors understand the structure of their institution's advancement functions and how that relates to their role and responsibilities as fundraisers?

- Are foundation board members knowledgeable about the memorandum of understanding between the foundation and the institution?

- Does the foundation board have knowledge of fundraising metrics from comparable institutions and expectations that are consistent with the constituency of their particular institution?

CASE STUDY

BUILDING THE FOUNDATION'S FUNDRAISING PROGRAM:
NORTHAMPTON COMMUNITY COLLEGE FOUNDATION

Northampton Community College, founded in 1967, serves more than 36,000 students at its main campus in Bethlehem, Penn., a branch campus in Tannersville, Penn., and 50 satellite sites in four counties. The Northampton Community College Foundation is the college's fundraising arm. Susan K. Kubik has served NCC for 37 years, including in the roles of vice president for institutional advancement and executive director of the foundation. (In 2011, Kubik announced her planned retirement in 2012.)

Over the years, the foundation has become increasingly crucial to NCC. Since 1976, the endowment has grown to $30 million, and the foundation has given the college more than $25 million for facilities, scholarships, and programs. The foundation also owns residence halls, which community colleges in Pennsylvania cannot own directly.

Like many community colleges, NCC's program began with fundraising events, but Kubik soon recognized the need to build a major gifts program. Armed with benchmark data, she approached the foundation board to support additional positions. Development staff members are employees of the college, but the foundation funds the equivalent of three positions. The investment has been rewarded: NCC's first campaign, in the 1980s, raised $3.5 million. The most recent campaign, concluded in 2007, raised $14.2 million against a goal of $13.5 million. The campaign total included four seven-figure gifts.

NCC initiated alumni programs in 1975, early in its history. Kubik notes that it takes time for an investment in alumni relations to be reflected in giving, but that a long-term approach pays off. Alumni gifts accounted for 20 percent of the most recent campaign. The foundation also launched planned giving 20 years ago and now realizes the benefits of that long-term investment, receiving bequests on a regular basis.

The foundation board—which Kubik describes as "one of the boards to be on in this community"—is extensively involved in the cultivation and solicitation of gifts. Volunteers solicited three of the seven-figure campaign gifts. Parents of students and community leaders who recognize the college's local impact also have been central as donors and volunteers.

Kubik's advice to other community-college foundations is to make a realistic assessment of the prospects available in their communities and build their fundraising programs accordingly. Those located near corporate or foundation headquarters may emphasize fundraising from those sources; others will do best to emphasize individual donors. Events may be a useful tool for some, but should not be the only method of fundraising. Most importantly, she emphasizes the need to "focus on the long-term development of relationships, not just year-to-year fundraising totals."

CHAPTER 3

THE FUNDRAISING TEAM

Effective fundraising is not a solo endeavor. It requires a team effort, in which all the players meet specific responsibilities. This chapter considers the fundraising team, summarizes what some other authors and studies have had to say about it, and then applies the model to the specific case of a public college or university with an institutionally related foundation, using insights from the 2010 AGB survey. Chapter 4 considers how foundation boards prepare and organize themselves to become effective in fundraising, and Chapter 5 then explores the details of foundation directors' involvement in fundraising activities, as reported by foundation chief executives in the 2010 AGB survey. Chapter 6 focuses on the role of the foundation board in the special situation of a campaign.

DEFINING THE FUNDRAISING TEAM

Various authors over the years, including board leaders, development professionals, and consultants, have described the ideal fundraising team and agree that the three key players are the board, the president, and the advancement or development professional—usually the chief advancement officer. Of course, at a public college or university the team is more complex, including the foundation board, the foundation chief executive officer (who may not be the same person as the chief advancement officer of the institution), and other players. But let's start with the three-party relationship that many authors describe and then add the complexity of public higher education to the model. It is important to emphasize that the discussion here is focused on the board's role related to *fundraising* and does not consider other aspects of the board's work, such as managing funds or other fiduciary responsibilities.

In the 1980s, William A. Kinnison and Michael J. Ferin compiled a list of responsibilities of fundraising team members that has stood the test of time. In *Fundraising Leadership: A Guide for University and College Boards* (AGB 1989), Kinnison and Ferin wrote that the board's responsibilities are:

- to ensure that fundraising efforts align with the mission and priorities of the institution;
- to monitor the fundraising operation (its budget and staff) to maximize revenue potential;
- to coordinate board-member fundraising activity with the president and chief advancement officer; and
- to be personally involved in the fundraising process.

The president's partnership responsibilities, they write, are:
- to provide leadership in defining and articulating the college's mission and to set priorities;
- to forge links between the board and advancement professionals;
- to provide support for board fundraising activities; and
- to be personally involved in the fundraising process.

Finally, according to Kinnison and Ferin, the responsibilities of the chief advancement officer are:
- to facilitate and enable the participation of board members and the president in the fundraising process by providing information, training, and preparatory work;
- to provide an effective teamwork environment;
- to translate mission, priority, and need into readily usable case statements and plans of action; and
- to be personally involved in the fundraising process.

FROM JOB DESCRIPTIONS TO GAME PLAN

Job descriptions are helpful, but they itemize the responsibilities of each player without saying much about how their roles interact in practice. When it comes to how they work together to raise money, it may be useful to think about another kind of team and how it functions when the game is being played.

In *Securing the Future*, published by AGB in 2005, I described the workings of the fundraising team through the metaphor of a football team. Baseball, basketball, and soccer are great sports, but I think football has characteristics that make it most like fundraising. Baseball and basketball emphasize individual performance; it is possible for an individual to put points on the board through heroic achievements. But in football, as in fundraising, scoring points usually requires the coordinated, simultaneous action of multiple players. There rarely is a fundraising equivalent to a three-point shot or a home run. And in fundraising, like in football, successes may be realized as intermediate steps in the game even before the team scores. For example, achieving a first down is a reason for the fans to cheer—it's an important milestone. Similarly, in fundraising, an initiative that begins or advances a relationship with a donor is a measureable achievement, even if a gift is not obtained on that play.

- **Fundraising is one of the only functions in which board members are asked to go beyond their policymaking role and become involved in carrying out activities.**

- **If resources are raised through private support and the foundation has responsibility for fundraising, both the foundation board and the governing board must work together.**

- **Some ways to achieve a healthy governing board/ foundation board relationship include, among others: creating orientation programs for both boards, appointing governing board members to the foundation board, and creating a joint planning committee of governing and foundation board members.**

- **Another responsibility for foundation board members is to establish goals and expectations and then monitor and evaluate the fundraising program.**

- **The metrics that the board will track should be a topic of discussion between the chief development officer or foundation executive and the board, resulting in agreement on perhaps a dozen key indicators to be reviewed by the board regularly.**

- **It is most appropriate to view fundraising as an investment and use a long-term horizon in evaluating its return.**

The roles of the central players on the fundraising team also have analogs in football. Looking back at Kinnison's and Ferin's list of board responsibilities above, the board members are the team's owners. They are focused on the overall success and sustainability of the enterprise. They set the standards for team performance and monitor results. But what makes this football team distinct is the expectation that, on the day of the game, the owners (board members) will come down from their sky boxes and engage in the game on the field—that is, that they will become "personally involved in the fundraising process." Indeed, fundraising is one of the only functions in which board members are asked to go beyond their policymaking role and become deeply involved in carrying out activities.

On the fundraising team, the institution's president holds down three jobs at once. He or she may be a member of the board, and thus an "owner," but the president is also the coach—leading, guiding, and sometimes pushing the board and other members of the team in their game performance. The president also is the team's star running back. That is, in addition to inspiring the team, training the other players, and developing the game plan, the president also must run the ball on many occasions and will be among the most visible players on the field—cheered by the fans on winning days and booed when the game goes south.

The president is often the person most able to advance the ball (that is, the institution's cause) and may be the most visible and applauded member of the team. But the whole game unfolds according to a plan, and each player respects and adheres to the game plan designed by the president in his or her role as coach. This point is crucial: Successful fundraising requires a plan that pulls together the contributions of all the players in an organized, coordinated way. Some presidents sometimes may be inclined to run the ball alone. But anyone who has played on a team with a player who hogs the ball will recognize that such a player often engenders resentment from teammates. Some presidents may be drawn to the idea of single-handedly securing the largest gifts and achieving acclaim from the faculty and the board, but they should remember that while a ball hog may be a star when the team is winning, he will receive the blame when there is a loss.

The chief advancement officer is the quarterback who calls the plays. He or she may sometimes run the ball but often hands it off or passes it to other members of the team. The chief advancement officer's role is complicated, too, in that fellow players (that is, the board and the president) are also the owners and the coach. The chief advancement officer may work for the president or the owners, but he or she also sometimes needs to push the president and the owners to high performance as members of the fundraising team. As in the NFL, the best fundraising quarterbacks are intensely recruited and well compensated, but they face high performance expectations.

Some chief advancement officers may be ball hoggers, too. Indeed, as discussed in Chapter 2, many development programs have become staff-driven in recent years, with development officers often soliciting gifts at significant levels. But chief advancement officers should remember that when quarterbacks try to run alone without a team around them, they might gain yardage, but they might get sacked instead. In fundraising as in football, it is best to keep the focus on overall team performance, sharing both the celebrations of success and the responsibility for inevitable disappointments.

Of course—to continue the football metaphor—other people are in the stadium. On one occasion several years ago, in my role as a consultant, I was invited by the system chancellor to speak to a gathering in Albany of the presidents and chief advancement officers of all 64 campuses that are part of the State University of New York. In my remarks, I described the football metaphor. When I finished, the chancellor asked me, "So what is the role of the SUNY system administration?" I replied, "You're the NFL; you establish the rules by which the teams can play." There was laughter, then one of the presidents asked, "And what is the position played by fundraising consultants?" I hesitated, so he proceeded to offer an answer to the question: "I think they're like the sports commentators; they're always talking, but they don't have any influence on the game itself." I thought it was a pretty good joke—and perhaps an accurate observation.

In sum, fundraising today is a professional sport, not a game to be played by amateurs on a sandlot without proper equipment, experience, and talent. That is to say, the stakes for colleges and universities are high, and an effective fundraising program—whether in times of a campaign or not—needs to be a sophisticated team effort to ensure efficiency, thoroughness, and effectiveness.

BOARD MEMBERS AS OWNERS

Looking back at Kinnison's and Ferin's list of responsibilities for boards, and continuing to apply the football-team metaphor, some activities are related to the role of owners, and others are related to being players on the field. The owners' work includes ensuring that fundraising priorities are aligned with institutional mission and priorities, and monitoring fundraising operations and performance. Becoming personally involved in fundraising and coordinating with the president and chief advancement officer are equivalent to playing the game and following the game plan. Let's look first at the board's ownership responsibilities and then at the board's involvement as players in the fundraising game.

Of course, Kinnison and Ferin write from the perspective of independent colleges and universities, where both owner and player responsibilities are placed in a single board. Indeed, much of the literature of educational fundraising assumes, or asserts, that governing and fundraising are inseparable. Some suggest that the board's responsibility to engage in fundraising is an extension of its overall fiduciary responsibility to sustain and advance the institution that it serves. Others say that board members' fiduciary responsibility for the institution and their engagement with the substance of its operations and programs are what motivate them to become generous donors and advocates for the college or university.

But many public colleges and universities have two boards: a governing board responsible for mission, academic priorities, and the overall welfare of the institution; and a foundation board responsible for fundraising and the management of private gifts. In this environment, who performs the owners' work of assuring alignment of institutional and fundraising priorities and setting fundraising goals consistent with such alignment? And who monitors the performance of the fundraising team members, some of whom may be officers of the institution and accountable to an institutional board, and others who may be employees of the foundation, accountable to the foundation CEO or board? The 2010 AGB survey was designed in part to add some light on these important questions. The findings will be presented later in this chapter. But, first, let's explore some of the details—and complexities—that are inherent in the owners' responsibilities.

MISSION AND ACADEMIC PRIORITIES

The mission and academic priorities of the institution are the responsibility of the board that governs it, subject to any public mandates that may apply. The missions of most colleges and universities are stated broadly to encompass the creation and transmission of knowledge. Yet beyond those general purposes, specific institutions also may have other important aspects to their missions, such as serving particular communities or specific categories of students.

Clearly, the institutional governing board has the overriding fiduciary responsibility—indeed, a legal as well as a moral responsibility—to ensure that everything the college or university does is consistent with its mission. Boards may be guided by a vision articulated by the president and priorities developed by the administration, but the governing board has the ultimate responsibility to ensure adherence to the institution's mission and the allocation of resources consistent with that mission. But if some of those resources are to be raised through private support, and the foundation has responsibility for fundraising, the two boards need to work together.

What might go wrong and how can problems be avoided? In *College and University Foundations: Serving America's Public Higher Education* (AGB 1997), by Joseph F. Phelan, AGB President Richard D. Legon provides some examples and proposes ways of avoiding conflict between the two boards.

In one of Legon's hypothetical examples, a new president decides that construction of a campus center is important to bring the community together. The vice president for advancement and some members of the governing board agree. The president approaches the foundation, which has been working from a five-year plan that emphasizes fundraising for academic program priorities, such as endowed chairs and scholarships. The foundation's fundraising consultant advises that it would be difficult to raise gift money for the new campus center, and the foundation board votes the project down. As Legon describes the unpleasant outcome: "The project is shelved. The vice president's professional life is shortened." And the new president has suffered disappointment and embarrassment.

In another hypothetical case described by Legon, a foundation board member persuades the president that a major new athletic facility should be built and that the foundation can raise the needed funds. The governing board is also persuaded and approves the project. But the bids exceed internal estimates, the foundation's fundraising falls short, and public controversy ensues.

In Legon's third (and perhaps scariest) scenario, foundation directors become frustrated with the president's fundraising performance. They become critical of the governing board's inattention to the issue and threaten to withhold foundation funds until the institution's board acts. Eventually the president resigns.

Because of their shared responsibility for the owners' work, the relationship between the governing board of the institution and the foundation board is crucial. Despite the existence of written understandings, the relationship requires effort. As Legon suggests, "A healthy governing board-foundation board relationship is marked by mutual respect and a clear understanding of shared, distinctive, and complementary responsibilities." His recommendations for achieving such a relationship include maintaining orientation programs for both boards to help clarify their roles, appointing some governing board members to the foundation board, establishing a development committee of the governing board, sharing the foundation's annual report and audit with the governing board, and creating a joint planning committee composed of members of both the governing board and the foundation board. Legon also calls for a strong leadership role for the president: "The president is responsible for promoting successful communications between the boards and creating a process to establish realistic funding priorities."

Most colleges and universities today engage in some form of strategic planning, usually through a process driven by the administration but with participation from other members of the campus community. In many instances, that planning produces a set of academic goals that are then translated into specific fundraising priorities, which form the basis for a campaign.

At a public institution, the governing board has the authority to adopt the institutional strategic plan and ensuring its consistency with the mission and the public interest. But if the plan envisions private support as a strategy for accomplishing objectives, the foundation shares responsibility for its success.

The process for identifying fundraising priorities should be inclusive and iterative. Legon suggests that the president establish a collaborative planning approach that involves the chairs of both boards and the foundation's chief executive, as well as other people throughout the campus. The resulting priorities are then discussed with the governing board, which may suggest refinements and determine which can be addressed with institutional funds or public dollars and which may require philanthropy. The next stop is the foundation board, which does a reality check on the proposed fundraising priorities. If the foundation directors think that some of the plan's priorities cannot be met through private support, they so advise the governing board and the president. As Legon suggests, it sometimes may be useful to conduct a feasibility study, sponsored jointly by the two boards, to further inform the planning process. A revised plan then goes back to the governing board for formal approval, with the foundation board signed on to the fundraising priorities it includes.

Achieving the desired consensus requires leadership from the institution's president or chancellor and also from the foundation's chief executive officer. Legon notes that having the foundation chief executive also serve as an officer of the institution, usually the chief advancement officer, may facilitate that leadership. As discussed in Chapter 1, that is the case in just over one-half of the foundations responding to the 2010 AGB survey. In cases where the positions are held by different people, additional communication and collaboration are clearly needed.

The shared responsibilities of foundation and governing boards may become even more sensitive as private support becomes increasingly important to public colleges and universities. The greatest need will be to balance the foundation's leadership with the prerogatives of the institution's president and governing board for setting academic priorities and policy.

Writing in the July/August 2008 issue of *Trusteeship*, Gary Bloom, a software executive and chair of the foundation board at California Polytechnic State University, describes the foundation board's efforts to have greater impact. He is clear about the limits as well as the foundation's evolving role: "I am not suggesting it's the job of a university foundation's board to run the university. Boards on university foundations with huge assets may be tempted to try to influence decisions they disagree with, but I don't think that's healthy. We do want to nudge the university sometimes to influence leaders in a direction that we think they need to go." He continues, "Among other things, [our] foundation challenged institutional leaders to revisit the university's vision and mission statement to incorporate what the university should look like 8 to 10 years from now."

Also writing in *Trusteeship*, in the September/October 2006 issue, Dave Frohnmayer, president of the University of Oregon, provides another perspective: "A foundation can come to see the funds it raises as its own and a university and a foundation can become antagonistic rivals instead of mutually supportive partners." Frohnmayer emphasizes that the president reports to the institutional governing board and must respond to that board's priorities. But "a foundation board may attempt to force itself into the governance arena by seeking control of the university's philanthropic capacity." The president may be torn—he or she wants to see the most influential and able individuals recruited to the foundation board, but "such individuals…may become frustrated by the limits on their authority."

Frohnmayer's proposed solution to this potential tension is a "shared vision for the partnership that is endorsed by the university and its president as well as by the foundation and its leadership...that relies on intentional connection and collaboration."

To some observers, the relationship between governance and philanthropy is a concern not confined to public institutions and related foundations. For example, Harvard University professor and board expert Richard Chait, in a July/August 2009 interview in *Trusteeship*, describes "the allure of philanthropy over governance" as "a gremlin" threatening governing board performance. His concerns include the emphasis given to wealth in recruiting board members, the tendency of boards to select leading donors as their leaders, the fact that major donors on the board may speak with a "louder voice" and thus have disproportionate influence on board decision making, and the potential loss of collegiality and cohesiveness that could arise from having some board members who are selected primarily for their wealth. Chait even suggests that financial support from governing board members could be viewed as a "conflict of interest" and notes that gifts from board members are considered unethical behavior in the Netherlands.

Although Chait mentions public institutions' increased reliance on private support as an issue, he seems to be primarily concerned about boards of private colleges and universities, where the responsibilities for governance and philanthropy are concurrent in a single board—the institution's governing board. One could argue that the formal structure at many public institutions provides an antidote to his concerns since the responsibility for governing of the institution is that of the institution's board, and the responsibility for providing and securing philanthropic support rests with the foundation board. That is a division of responsibility that would appear to neutralize the "gremlin" that worries Chait.

But, in reality, major sources of support—whether they are private donors or the state legislature—always have had an influence on the decisions of institutional governing boards. As private support, channeled through institutionally related foundations, becomes a larger component of revenue at public institutions, it is inevitable that donors and foundation directors will have at least some opinion on institutional policy and programs that will need to be considered. As will be discussed at other points in this book, there is a connection between a person's involvement in the substance of the institution's programs—and perhaps his or her sense of responsibility that comes from holding a decision-making role—and that person's motivation to give. And, especially in today's environment, few donors are willing to give and walk away, eschewing any voice in the decisions about how their resources will be applied. Chait does "not think philanthropy would plummet merely because major donors no longer had seats in the boardroom." But that overlooks the point that having at least a voice in institutional policy often enhances the desire to become a major donor. In other words, the psychological dynamics may sometimes lead in a direction opposite from what Chait would prefer.

Of course, there is a need to maintain an awareness of the pitfalls and to ensure, as Frohnmayer suggests, "a shared vision." And of course there is a need to consciously maintain an appropriate balance and a clear and mutual understanding about respective roles. But adoption of the culture of the Netherlands in American higher education would be ironic at a time when universities around the world are striving to emulate the U.S. model of public-private partnerships in support of higher education.

MONITORING AND EVALUATING FUNDRAISING

Establishing goals and expectations and then monitoring and evaluating the fundraising program is owners' work, too. Of course, maintaining appropriate balance is again important. When owners of football teams become too involved and second-guess their coaches, the result is often rancorous relationships and losing teams.

It is not always easy for a board to monitor performance of the fundraising program or members of the team with total confidence. The situation is perhaps easier during a campaign, when reports show progress toward campaign objectives that can be measured against specific targets and deadlines in the campaign plan. But if the institution is not in a campaign, it becomes more difficult to know exactly what numbers should be used to evaluate fundraising progress.

The most obvious standard is, of course, dollars; after all, that is what fundraising is ultimately about. One caution is that the board should not focus exclusively on year-to-year changes in gift totals. Because major gifts can cause results to fluctuate widely from year to year, it is more realistic to measure growth over longer periods—perhaps using three-year averages of gifts arrayed by source and purpose. Another common method of smoothing out the fluctuations caused by major gifts—to create a more accurate picture of changes in baseline support—is to eliminate the three largest gifts from the annual totals before comparing the changes.

Even when properly presented and interpreted, gift totals may not provide an adequate measure of whether the institution's fundraising program is meeting long-term goals. It may be useful to review additional metrics, tailored to the institution's particular needs and circumstances. For example, the rate of alumni participation may be important at a college or university that has the goal of broadening its base of support. In addition, measures of gifts in the pipeline, such as known bequest intentions, may be worth tracking to gain a sense of future gift revenue.

The chief advancement officer or the foundation CEO is likely to be using additional metrics in managing the development program and staff, and the board owners may be interested in some of those measures to gauge how effectively staff and resources are being deployed. While the board should not become absorbed in the daily operations of the development office, it may be appropriate for it to receive reports concerning, for example, the number of visits to major gift prospects the development staff completes each month—including cultivation visits, solicitations, and visits related to qualifying new prospects. The board may monitor the full range of the office's activity by learning the number of proposals submitted to private foundations and corporations at various levels, the number of planned-giving illustrations prepared, and other operational metrics. In other words, it is appropriate for the board to have at its disposal more information than simple win-loss statistics.

Again, the board should not review all of the management reports that the chief advancement officer or foundation chief executive may use in running the development operation. Instead, the subject of which metrics the board will track should be a topic of discussion between the chief development officer or foundation executive and the board, resulting in agreement on perhaps a dozen key indicators that will be reviewed by the board on a regular basis.

Understandably and appropriately, the board will be concerned with the costs of raising money. However, determining the appropriate investment in fundraising and measuring the return on that investment are not always simple matters. Expenditure data from the few national studies that have been conducted in the past may be of limited usefulness for comparison. In 2010, the Council for Advancement and Support of Education (CASE) launched a new study to examine advancement costs, which may provide boards with more helpful data. In addition, many colleges and universities belong to organizations of peers that collect data useful for benchmarking.

The board should examine fundraising costs with three important points in mind. First, when looking at benchmark data, are apples being compared with apples? For example, are the fundraising costs of the benchmarked institutions fully loaded—that is, has institutional overhead attributable to the development operation been included in the figures? If a foundation is served by both its own staff and institutional staff, have all relevant institutional expenses been included in the calculation? Especially in decentralized programs, are hidden costs buried in the budgets of colleges, schools, and other units that may be captured at some institutions but not at others?

Second, the commonly used standard of cost-per-dollar-raised may be at best misleading. Looking at the return on investment in fundraising often presents a different picture, even when the same figures are used. For example, a cost of 50 cents per dollar raised may sound high, but what investor would find it unattractive to double his or her money in a year? If the development office is viewed as a cost center, the institution or the foundation is likely to under-invest in its programs, and fundraising is thus not likely to achieve its full potential. It is more productive to view fundraising as an investment and use a long-term horizon in evaluating its return.

It may be instructive for the board to examine costs disaggregated by various fundraising programs—for example, annual giving, planned giving, and major gifts—as well as the overall return on investment in the fundraising effort. It is essential to measure program costs over at least a three-year period, recognizing that new initiatives take time to become effective and that year-to-year fluctuations may occur even in established programs.

The third point to keep in mind in gauging fundraising costs is that comparisons among various institutions—even those within some defined group of peers—must consider the full dimensions of each institution's fundraising environment and history. In other words, the variables relevant to fundraising—not the characteristics that define peers in such areas as athletics or academics—should determine the peer group for benchmarking fundraising costs.

For example, a college that historically has prepared students for careers in education may have fewer prospects for major gifts than one of similar size that has historically graduated majors in business, even if both institutions are of similar size and now offer similar academic programs. Because it receives fewer major gifts, the former institution may be spending relatively more to attract such gifts. Also, it may appropriately be spending more in its annual fund program because it is investing in building a tradition of giving that will pay dividends in future years. Thus, having different histories and traditions may make two seemingly comparable institutions very different from one another in how they are positioned for fundraising.

Too often, board leaders who understand the relationship between risk and reward in their own business endeavors become too cautious when they move into the higher education boardroom and focus excessively on minimizing expenses without full confidence in the returns that fundraising is likely to provide. As Charles Steger, the president of Virginia Tech, describes it in the May/June 2000 issue of *Trusteeship*): "Everybody wants to go to heaven, but nobody wants to die. [In other words,] everyone wants to reach the campaign's goals, but no one wants to pay the necessary costs."

Some authors include in the list of the board's responsibilities, as a part of its overall monitoring function, evaluation of the president's fundraising performance. That is pretty straightforward at independent colleges and universities, where the board may assess the president's fundraising as a part of its overall evaluation. Since the president of a public college or university reports to the institution's governing board, that board is in the formal position to perform that particular ownership role. But if the foundation board is responsible for fundraising and the institution's board is not involved, the latter may have inadequate information with which to make a judgment without input from the foundation board. If the foundation CEO is also an officer of the institution, the foundation board may have an opinion about his or her performance, but the authority to evaluate that person is shared with the president. There must be a clear understanding of lines of authority. The foundation board may provide input, but it must fully understand and respect the authority of the institution's governing board and the president.

OWNERS IN THE PUBLIC-INSTITUTION STADIUM

As discussed above, the rules of the game may be complex in the case of a public institution with a foundation. Ownership work is shared between the institution's governing board and the board of the foundation. The foundation chief executive may or may not be an officer of the institution itself. How is the fundraising game actually played in this stadium? In order to gain insight on that question, the 2010 AGB survey asked foundation chief executives to identify which party—the foundation board, the foundation CEO, the institution's governing board, the institution's CEO (president or chancellor), or the foundation's CAO—is primarily responsible for several key activities. The results are summarized in Table 3.1.

Table 3.1: Who is Primarily Responsible?
(% of foundation CEO responses)

	Foundation Board	Foundation CEO	Institution Board	Institution CEO	Institution CAO	We don't do/have
Ensuring that fundraising priorities align with institutional priorities	7.7%	51.5%	0.0%	10.0%	30.8%	0.0%
Establishing fundraising goals (outside of a campaign)	22.7%	38.6%	0.8%	14.4%	22.7%	0.8%
Establishing naming policies regarding buildings, academic units, endowed positions, etc.	10.8%	11.5%	40.8%	15.4%	20.0%	1.5%
Developing gift-acceptance policies	46.2%	30.0%	1.5%	1.5%	20.8%	0.0%
Establishing investment and fund-management policies	90.9%	6.0%	1.5%	0.8%	0.0%	0.8%
Setting the metrics by which fundraising performance will be evaluated	19.7%	36.4%	0.8%	8.3%	28.8%	6.0%
Monitoring fundraising performance (e.g., receiving and discussing regular reports)	23.7%	42.0%	1.5%	2.3%	29.8%	0.8%
Evaluating the fundraising performance of the institution's president/chancellor	3.8%	3.1%	43.8%	0.0%	2.3%	46.9%
Evaluating the performance of the foundation CEO	50.8%	0.0%	2.3%	34.4%	3.9%	8.6%
Evaluating the performance of the institution's chief advancement officer	3.1%	7.8%	0.8%	59.7%	7.0%	21.7%
Evaluating the fundraising performance of the foundation board	34.9%	11.6%	1.6%	0.8%	5.4%	45.7%

Two reminders are important: The data in Table 3.1 reflect what is actually occurring and do not represent recommended best practices. Second, the survey was completed by foundation chief executives, so the data reflect only that perspective.

Many of the responses shown in Table 3.1 suggest a relatively clear division of responsibilities and are consistent with what we might expect. For example, it is understandable that, in most cases, the institution's governing board (40.8 percent), the institution's CEO (15.4 percent), or the chief advancement officer (20.0 percent) is primarily responsible for establishing policies regarding the naming of buildings, academic units, and endowed positions—those are things that the institution owns and for which it has responsibility. In the largest number of cases, the president's fundraising performance is not formally evaluated (46.9 percent), but when it is, the evaluation unsurprisingly is most often conducted by the governing board, to which the president reports (43.8 percent).

Likewise, it makes sense that foundation boards (46.2 percent) and foundation CEOs (30.0 percent) are usually the ones who determine gift-acceptance policies, and that foundation boards almost always set policies for the management and investment of gift funds (90.9 percent). The foundation receives and manages the funds, and it is the responsibility of its board to ensure that sound practices are followed and excessive risks are avoided.

In addition, study responses showing that most foundation CEOs are evaluated by their boards (50.8 percent), and most institution chief advancement officers by their presidents (59.7 percent), are consistent with what might be expected, although they do not fully describe the complexity in cases where those positions are held by the same person.

But some of the data in Table 3.1 reveal interesting ambiguities. For example, ensuring that fundraising priorities align with institutional priorities—an owner's responsibility as discussed earlier in this chapter—is in the majority of cases primarily the responsibility of the foundation CEO (51.5 percent) or the institution's chief advancement officer (30.8 percent). The foundation board is reported as primarily responsible for ensuring such alignment in fewer than 8 percent of cases. No survey respondents identified the institution board as having the primary responsibility in this regard, although that board has ultimate responsibility for priorities of the institution and thus a stake in ensuring that resources are available to pursue them.

What emerges quite clearly from Table 3.1 is the central role played by foundation chief executives and institution chief advancement officers, which may be, of course, an overlapping category in about half of the cases. In the largest number of cases, foundation CEOs are primarily responsible for establishing the metrics by which fundraising performance will be evaluated (36.4 percent), and for monitoring fundraising performance (42.0 percent). Less than a quarter of foundation boards are reported to be primarily responsible for those activities and, again, institution governing boards appear to play little role in what would seem to be important ownership functions.

It is also interesting that the largest portion of foundation boards (45.7 percent) are not evaluated on their fundraising performance—by themselves or anyone else—although they are essential players on the fundraising field.

BOARD MEMBERS ON THE FIELD

As discussed above, in this unusual football game of fundraising, the owners are expected to play on the field during the game, participating in running, blocking, passing, and scoring points. The 2010 AGB survey also sought insights on the overall scenario in which foundation directors participate as fundraising athletes.

One can envision four hypothetical scenarios for the foundation board's participation in the cultivation and solicitation of major gift donors. In some situations, volunteer leaders are the primary fundraisers for the institution. This scenario might exist, for example, at a small or highly specialized institution lacking the capacity of a large advancement office and perhaps with a president who is deeply engaged in internal management. At the other extreme might be an entirely staff-driven program, in which a large major gifts staff makes most of the donor visits, and the board is minimally involved. That might be the case at a large university with thousands of prospects who are widely dispersed across the country, most of whom may not be well known to board members. In between are two scenarios in which trustees participate in limited ways as requested by the president and the advancement staff—one in which board members are primarily door-openers for visits by the president and advancement staff, and another in which they participate along with the president and/or a member of the advancement staff in some cultivation or solicitation activities. The last two scenarios would seem to reflect a team approach to fundraising, although with somewhat different roles played by the board.

In the 2010 AGB survey, foundation CEOs were asked to characterize the involvement of their boards in major gift fundraising according to the four scenarios. Their responses are summarized in Table 3.2. The most common response (50.4 percent) suggests a coordinated team approach in which board members participate in cultivation, solicitation, and stewardship activities, usually accompanied by the president or an advancement officer. The next highest response (31.1 percent) indicates that trustees play chiefly the role of opening doors for solicitations by the president and advancement staff. That is still a team approach, but it suggests a more limited board member role—in the football metaphor, that of offensive linemen who clear a path for the president and advancement staff to run the ball.

Another 14.8 percent of programs are predominantly staff driven, and foundation board members play no active role beyond providing their own financial support. (In our football game, they are essentially the fans.) That scenario may be more common at colleges and universities with large major gift staffs. In only 3.7 percent of instances does the foundation board provide the leadership in the cultivation, solicitation, and stewardship of major donors, a situation that may be typical only at small institutions with a limited number of professional development staff.

Again, as with most survey data, such numbers may be misleading because respondents interpret the questions in their own ways and without opportunities for clarification or feedback. Researchers are similarly biased in their interpretation of the responses. But one can infer from the responses that, at most institutions where foundation directors are engaged in fundraising, their participation in specific activities is at the request of, or at least is coordinated by, the institution's or foundation's staff. That seems consistent with the division of responsibilities envisioned in the football metaphor, with the chief advancement officer quarterbacking the plays carried out by board members.

It is interesting to compare the responses of foundation chief executives in the 2010 AGB survey with the responses of chief advancement officers at independent colleges and universities to an AGB survey directed to them in 2004, as reported in the book *Securing the Future*, published by AGB. The comparative percentages are displayed in Table 3.2. The data are separated by six years, so they are not directly comparable. But in general the pattern of responses suggests that where foundation boards have adopted an active role in fundraising, they partner with the staff in the same ways as their counterparts on independent-sector governing boards.

Table 3.2

Patterns of Involvement of Foundation Board Members in Major Gifts Fundraising

(Foundation chief executives were asked to select one statement that "most closely describes" major gifts fundraising at their foundation/institution.)

Characterization of board participation	2010 AGB survey (foundation CEO responses)	2004 AGB survey of independent colleges and universities
Fundraising is predominantly staff-driven. Foundation board members are expected to make personal gifts but nothing more.	14.8%	12.8%
Fundraising is primarily conducted by the institution president or the institution/ foundation development staff. Foundation board members are expected to help only by providing introductions and opening doors to prospects.	31.1%	23.2%
Foundation board members participate in some cultivation, stewardship, and solicitations, usually accompanied by the institution president or an institution/ foundation development staff person.	50.4%	56.0%
Members of the foundation board are deeply involved in fundraising and take leadership in the cultivation, solicitation, and stewardship of major donors.	3.7%	8.0%

WORKING TO ACHIEVE TEAMWORK

The division of responsibilities between the institution board and the foundation board requires clear definition and continuing communication and coordination—not only to avoid potential controversy but also to ensure that fundraising is aligned with institutional priorities and that the progress of the fundraising program is regularly evaluated. The 2010 AGB survey asked foundation CEOs to identify the mechanisms through which that is accomplished, producing the results shown in Table 3.3.

Table 3.3

**How the Foundation Board and Governing Board of the Institution
Coordinate and Communicate About Fundraising**

(Foundation CEOs identified which statement "best describes" how coordination is achieved.)

The institution chief development/advancement officer and/or the foundation CEO keeps both boards involved and informed.	32.5%
Overlapping members provide coordination and communication between the boards.	23.6%
The institution president keeps both boards involved and informed.	22.0%
Coordination and communication is informal; no particular process or structure is used to communicate with regard to fundraising.	19.5%
There is no coordination or communication.	2.4%

Table 3.3 highlights, again, the vital role of foundation CEOs and chief advancement officers as agents of communication and coordination between the boards. Given the complexities of the relationships involved, the position is one that requires a high degree of skill, judgment, and integrity. Presidents also play an important role in maintaining teamwork among the members of both boards in their role as coach.

The data in Table 3.3 also suggest that some of Richard D. Legon's recommendations, mentioned earlier, have been implemented. For example, overlapping membership between the institutional and foundation boards exists in about one-quarter of cases. (Special campaign committees also often include members of both boards; they are discussed in Chapter 6). About 20 percent of those surveyed report that communication and coordination are informal or nonexistent. That may be tolerable if the foundation is small and private support is not an important source of revenue to the institution. But if the role of the foundation is significant or if it increases, those institutions perhaps should consider more formalized ways of teambuilding. A small number, 2.4 percent, report no coordination or communication, a situation that could prove quite problematic if the foundation grows and its board becomes a more active participant in fundraising.

In addition to the shared vision that Frohnmayer recommends, some structure also may help to ensure congruence between institutional and foundation priorities. One example is the Joint Development Committee of the University of Iowa and the University of Iowa Foundation. While not a joint committee of the two boards—and *not to be confused with the development committee of the foundation board*, discussed in Chapter 4—this committee brings together the executive leadership of the university and the foundation and reinforces the finding of the central role played by the institution and foundation chief executives. (For more information, please see the case study on page 80.)

VOICES FROM THE FIELD

Representative comments offered by foundation chief executive officers about the fundraising team at their institutions/foundations:

"Our foundation board takes responsibility, but at the direction of the staff."

"The foundation board takes its cue from the university for priorities and needs. Then it helps to identify and cultivate potential donors."

"Our foundation board wants to take an active role in fundraising, but it needs better leadership from the institution."

"The foundation board should follow the institution strategic plan for fundraising and work with the institution to develop prospects and assist with the fundraising effort."

"The most important thing for foundation boards to do is to become educated about the needs of the institution."

"The most important thing the foundation CEO can do is to be sure that the institution and the foundation board are working together for the good of the institution."

"The foundation CEO should communicate regularly with the institution CEO on expectations for fundraising performance."

"The CEO needs to educate the board to understand the role of the foundation."

"Right now we have a very small staff and we are unable to support the board as we should. We aim to have a very involved board."

"Our board has the passion and commitment and wants to help the college. We need to make sure they have the tools they need."

Questions for Foundation Boards to Consider

- Is there sufficient teamwork and effective communication among the various players in the complex game of fundraising at the institution?

- Are foundation directors, the president, the governing board, the foundation CEO, the chief advancement officer, and development staff all clear on their differing but interlocking roles in fundraising?

- Is the institution/foundation investing enough in fundraising programs?

- Is the institution/foundation applying appropriate measures of fundraising effectiveness as compared with that of peer institutions?

- Is the institution's board informed about the importance of private support in achieving the mission and priorities that they have established for the institution?

- Are coordination and communication between the institutional board and the foundation board adequate to ensure that the ownership responsibilities that are shared between them are met in a coordinated and harmonious way?

- Are there formal structures or procedures for coordination between the executive leadership of the foundation and the institution?

CASE STUDY

ENSURING COMMUNICATION AND COORDINATION:
WASHBURN UNIVERSITY FOUNDATION

Established in 1865 and located in Topeka, Kan., Washburn is a publicly funded, independently governed, state-coordinated university. Washburn University enrolls 7,230 students in the college of arts and sciences and schools of applied studies, business, law, and nursing. The Washburn University Foundation is an independent organization that raises and manages private support and manages alumni records. JuliAnn Mazachek was appointed president of the foundation (then known as the Washburn Endowment Association) in 2002, having previously served as dean of Washburn's school of business.

The university is governed by a nine-member board of regents, with members appointed by the governor, the mayor of Topeka, the Shawnee County Commission, and the Kansas Board of Regents. The foundation has both a board of trustees and a smaller board of directors. The board of trustees, the members of which serve lifetime terms, nominate and elect members of the board of directors, who serve four-year terms and hold fiduciary responsibility for the foundation.

Washburn's complex environment, which includes multiple boards, requires communication and coordination to ensure that the foundation's fundraising priorities align with the university's academic plans.

Mazachek explains that the foundation's two-board model is helpful in this regard. The larger board of trustees not only provides opportunities to engage more volunteers but also ensures that individuals elected to the board of directors already have a good understanding of the foundation and its programs.

The need for communication is also addressed by having both the university president and the chair of the board of regents serve on the foundation board. The university president thus has multiple opportunities to communicate with the foundation board through participation in its meetings and retreats.

An additional vehicle for coordination is a liaison committee that includes the university and foundation presidents and the chair and vice chairs of both the board of regents and foundation board of directors. This committee regularly reviews academic priorities of the university and determines which can be addressed through philanthropy, establishing the foundation's fundraising priorities and goals for major projects and campaigns.

Mazachek emphasizes the importance of transparency, communication, and, especially, a solid relationship between the university and foundation presidents. "The foundation president's perspective is critical," she explains. "He or she needs to recognize that the foundation's role is to support the institution's strategic plan and academic priorities as determined by the university president and university governing board. The foundation does not determine the overarching priorities."

CHAPTER 4

PREPARING AND ORGANIZING THE BOARD FOR FUNDRAISING

B uilding a foundation board that can meet its fundraising responsibilities begins with identifying and enlisting potential directors with philanthropic capacity and inclination. It continues through the process of reaching explicit understandings with board members about the board's fundraising obligations and responsibilities. And it requires continuing work to create an environment in which foundation directors are mindful of the essential nature of their fundraising leadership and consistently focused on the need for philanthropic support. There is also a need for appropriate structure to lead the board's successful involvement in fundraising.

This chapter explores how fundraising and philanthropy are discussed in the process of enlisting new board members and how board leaders keep fundraising prominent in the board's thinking. It then describes the principal organizational structure through which many boards provide fundraising leadership—the development committee—and offers guidance on how the board chair, development committee chair, institution president, and foundation CEO can best create a climate in which the board is motivated to achieve its full fundraising potential.

IDENTIFYING BOARD MEMBERS OF AFFLUENCE AND INFLUENCE

If a foundation aspires to play an active role in fundraising, then the capacity to give and raise funds must be an important consideration in selecting who to serve on the board. In other words, it is essential to get the right people on the bus. The classic standard that board members should be recruited for "work, wealth, and wisdom" still requires that at least some of the directors be recruited primarily for their philanthropic capacity. And, of course, as J.W. Pocock wrote in the book *Fundraising Leadership* (AGB, 1989), "Wisdom and wealth...are not necessarily mutually exclusive adornments." While some directors may be recruited primarily for their expertise in investing funds, managing real estate, or some other aspect of the foundation's work, most are likely to be people of some affluence and influence who can play a role in giving and helping to obtain new resources.

Foundation CEOs' responses in the 2010 AGB survey, summarized in Table 4.1, suggest that the ability to give and willingness to participate in fundraising are indeed balanced with other considerations in selecting foundation board members. Almost one-half of the chief executives rated the ability to make a gift as very important; the willingness and ability to solicit gifts is very important in almost one-third of responses. Only about 20 percent of foundation executives say that willingness and ability to solicit gifts are not very important, and only 7.6 percent say that the ability to make a personal gift is unimportant.

As befits organizations that have responsibility for managing as well as raising funds, expertise in investments and other business activities is also highly valued in board members. And, as on most boards, both diversity and the personal compatibility of new members with existing board members are important considerations. The latter reflects more than the desire to create a friendly environment; it is probably essential to building an effective team. One interesting percentage shown in Table 4.1 pertains to the importance of the board candidate's relationship to the institution's governing board, which is "not very important" to a clear majority (63.4 percent) of foundations.

In the 2010 AGB survey, when foundation CEOs were asked their views on the criteria now used to identify new members of their foundation boards, 45.5 percent said they think the current criteria are about right. But the majority (54.5 percent) thinks there should be more emphasis on recruiting people who can give and raise funds. Unsurprisingly, none think that the ability to give and raise funds should be less of an emphasis than it is now.

Table 4.1
Importance of Criteria in Selecting Foundation Board Members

(% of foundation CEO responses)

	Very important	Somewhat important	Not very important
Ability to make a significant gift	45.5%	47.0%	7.6%
Willingness and ability to solicit gifts	31.1%	48.5%	20.5%
Expertise in managing investments	26.5%	58.3%	15.2%
Expertise in real estate, business ventures, etc.	12.9%	58.3%	28.8%
Personal compatibility with other board members	34.1%	51.5%	14.4%
Relationship with the institution's governing board	6.9%	29.8%	63.4%
Diversity/community representation	51.1%	41.2%	7.6%

TAKEAWAYS FOR FOUNDATION BOARD MEMBERS

- The capacity to give and raise funds must be an important consideration in selecting individuals to serve on a foundation board. At least some directors should be recruited primarily for their philanthropic capacity.

- Boards should learn about and be able to discuss the broad issues affecting philanthropy in higher education.

- The development committee of the board is responsible for providing leadership in fundraising, but it should not be viewed as the committee that does all the fundraising.

- Giving new board members a clear, upfront understanding of their responsibilities and expectations for giving is essential to avoiding future disappointments or misunderstandings.

- Board members should respect the professional knowledge and judgment of the advancement professionals and work together with them as a team.

Of course, some foundations will have access to more affluent prospective board members than will others, but the search for such people should be an ongoing effort. The identification of new board candidates is a responsibility of current directors, who should function as the foundation's talent scouts in their own business and professional circles. In addition, the development office, through its prospect-research operations, continually identifies affluent individuals within the institution's constituencies, and it can be helpful in bringing potential board members to the foundation's attention.

SETTING CLEAR EXPECTATIONS FROM THE OUTSET

Giving new board recruits a clear, upfront understanding of their responsibilities and expectations for giving is essential to avoiding future disappointments or misunderstandings. Inviting someone to join the board based on his or her professional skills or other qualities without any discussion of financial obligations risks setting up a negative reaction when that person subsequently is asked for a financial commitment. Indeed, most people invited to join a board are sophisticated and experienced individuals, who are likely to raise the question themselves if it is not addressed.

The 2010 AGB survey suggests that most foundation boards follow the practice of discussing giving expectations with new board members, with 69.9 percent of foundation CEOs saying that the giving and fundraising responsibilities of the board as a whole are always discussed in the recruitment process, and another 25.2 percent saying that the subject is sometimes discussed. Only 4.9 percent of foundation executives say that general expectations for board giving are never discussed in the process of recruiting new trustees. By comparison, AGB's 2004 survey of independent colleges and universities found that board giving expectations are always discussed during enlistment at 72.4 percent of institutions—a higher percentage, but not that different.

Preparing and Organizing the Board for Fundraising

In the 2010 survey, foundation CEOs were asked whether giving expectations for *individual* board members are discussed during enlistment. Of the total responding, 70.6 percent say that they always are discussed, 22.5 percent say that they are sometimes discussed, and 6.9 percent say that they never are discussed.

Views differ about exactly how to raise the subject of an individual's personal giving in the board-enlistment discussion and how to set the standards for what board members are expected to do. Prospective directors often will ask about the expected level of giving when they are invited to join the foundation board, and a variety of responses is possible. Moreover, some foundations have established formal policies on board giving, with minimum annual giving standards for directors. In this book, I offer my own opinions on these questions, based on my experience and reflection, although some foundation executives and advancement officers would probably disagree with me.

In the process of enlisting a new board member, I think it usually is inappropriate to propose a specific major gift. This converts the discussion into a solicitation and may create confusion about the purpose of the meeting. The prospective board member may be taken aback and feel that he or she is being asked to buy a seat on the board. It also means that a gift is being solicited before the person has had an opportunity to build an identity with the institution through involvement with the board's work. Any gift committed at this stage of the relationship may be much less than could be obtained after a longer period of cultivation.

Annual giving is, of course, a different matter, and the question of expectations might be handled in various ways. Citing the current average annual gift from board members might be one way to respond, but the range may be too wide to be helpful or instructive to a particular person. Moreover, citing the average could have the effect of lowering the sights of an individual with exceptional capacity. If the foundation board is trying to increase the giving capacity of the board overall by enlisting people of greater wealth, citing the current situation as a guideline would likely be a mistake.

Another approach when recruiting new board member might be to say that director gifts fall in several ranges. For example, some board members may make annual gifts in six figures, others in five-figures, and some lower—each according to his or her means. It is fair, of course, to also acknowledge—if such is the case—that some members of the board do not have significant financial capacity but nevertheless make modest contributions to the annual fund. Presented with this information, most prospective board members will have a sense of the landscape, identify which approach is most appropriate for them, and surmise what level of gift is most likely to be sought in the future. It addresses the question without becoming so specific that the invitation to join the board has turned into a solicitation. But it is still a little fuzzy.

Of course, some foundation boards have a specific policy on directors' giving. If such a policy exists, it provides a clear and ready answer to the question when it is asked by a prospective board member. Some boards require a minimum annual gift from board members. If that requirement exists, then it surely would need to be disclosed in the process of extending an invitation to join the board. Indeed, one downside of the required minimum gift is that it forces the enlistment conversation to be a solicitation as well. The subject of required minimum gifts is explored further in Chapter 5.

Regardless of the specific approach, it is essential that the subject of giving and participating in fundraising not be ignored in the enlistment of new trustees; the most likely results of such neglect include misunderstanding and disappointment.

CREATING AN ENVIRONMENT FOR BOARD LEADERSHIP

Assuming that foundation directors are enlisted with a clear understanding of their responsibilities to give and to participate in fundraising, it also is important to maintain the board's focus on the subject through regular discussions at board meetings and in other settings. Fundraising should be part of the agenda in orienting new trustees, in board self-studies, and at board retreats.

Of course, most directors do not join the foundation board only to give and raise money; they are likely to become deeply interested in other work of the board, the foundation, and the institution. Unless a discussion of fundraising is a part of every board meeting, there is the risk that foundation directors will begin to lose sight of their own role and come to view it as something the president or the advancement staff does, rather than a central aspect of the board's own responsibility.

FOCUS ON BOARD GIVING PERFORMANCE

The board chair and foundation CEO should take the lead in ensuring that a discussion of fundraising is a part of every meeting of the full board and in setting the right tone. In the 2010 AGB survey, 82.5 percent of foundation chief executives say that reports on overall fundraising progress are always presented at board meetings, while another 17.5 percent say such reports are sometimes presented. (None say that they never are presented.) But board giving in particular appears to be less often a focus at board meetings. Of the foundation CEOs who say that fundraising reports are presented to the board, only 24.5 percent say that the reports always break out board giving as a distinctive category. Another 29.4 percent say that board giving is sometimes broken out in such reports. The largest number, 46.1 percent, say that board giving is never shown separately in reports presented to the board.

Some believe that presenting a summary of board giving at every meeting is important because it puts the subject out in the open and keeps board members focused on their financial obligations. In my opinion, this generally is a sound principle. But in reality, there may be circumstances in which doing so could have a negative impact. For example, if some board members are giving generously while others are not, calling attention to the board's poor giving overall could have a negative impact on those who are doing their share. Such deficiencies in board performance are a real problem, but they need to be addressed in a way that does not adversely affect the morale of the board—especially among those members who are meeting their commitments.

Of course, if the board is performing well in giving and in fundraising, that should be cause for congratulations from the chair and expressions of gratitude from the president and the foundation CEO. It also can be useful for the board chair and the president or foundation chief executive to acknowledge particularly generous directors in front of their peers at board meetings. It is a rare individual who does not appreciate such recognition, and providing it helps raise the sights of others.

However, in my view, the full board meeting may not be the right place to discuss inadequate giving by the board or some of its members. I have observed board chairs direct a general scolding to the board as a whole during a meeting. That is likely to set a negative tone and have little benefit. Statements that paint with a broad brush may be resented by directors who already are giving their fair share but are nevertheless forced to listen to lectures about how the board should do more. When their awareness of nonperformance by other members is increased in this way, some who are giving now may think the situation unfair and reduce their own support. Those who are not giving what they could and should may feel embarrassed, even if they are not identified by name. That is not likely to make them feel more inclined to give and may even lead to dissension and resignations.

It is better for discussions in the board meeting to be kept positive, while the board chair, development committee chair, or foundation CEO address concerns about any directors who are not meeting expectations in one-on-one conversations with those individuals. To cite John Pocock's 1989 book again: "No general call for funds or fervent exhortation from the board chair can rouse [board members] to give to the hilt. [Board members], too, are individuals and, along with all major prospects, should expect personal attention."

ESTABLISHING A BOARD POLICY ON FUNDRAISING

Some suggest that the board adopt a formal policy on board participation in giving and fundraising. Such a policy may help to make fundraising a fixed part of the board's culture. It might not only state clearly that the board is responsible for ensuring adequate private support, but also set specific expectations for personal financial support among board members. (Again, that topic will be explored further in Chapter 5.)

AGB's book *Margin of Excellence*, published in 2005, includes a list of responsibilities of foundation board members that might be considered for adoption as a policy or at least for inclusion in the board's manual. Among other responsibilities of foundation board members are the following that relate directly to giving and participation in fundraising:

• Set an example through personal giving (annual giving and periodic campaigns);

• Encourage donor participation and ensure donor confidence;

• Identify and cultivate prospects (help open doors);

• Solicit gifts; and

• Encourage the proper acknowledgment of gifts and donors.

I believe that adopting a formal policy does no harm and may help to increase the board's awareness of its responsibilities; for example, the policy may be a useful part of the briefing packet given new trustees. However, no policy can substitute for continuous, live discussion of fundraising by the board—or for the board chair and development committee chair keeping the need for philanthropy always on the board agenda.

EDUCATING THE BOARD ABOUT PHILANTHROPY

In addition to specific discussions about the board's own performance in giving and fundraising, it is important to provide the board with opportunities to learn more about and discuss the broad issues affecting philanthropy in higher education. This helps put both the board's performance and its expectations for the president, foundation CEO, and development staff into realistic perspective. Topics for discussion might include: trends in philanthropy, changing laws affecting planned giving, ethical issues and policies regarding donor involvement and corporate partnerships, donor privacy issues, and other subjects of current interest and controversy.

As former AGB President Richard T. Ingram wrote in the March 2004 issue of *Currents*, "Such conversations too often get tabled during committee and board meetings already laden with too-crowded agendas." These discussions should, of course, be a part of the development committee's meetings, but they also should also take place during full board meetings and board retreats. Retreats are intended as opportunities for the board to reflect on larger environmental and strategic issues. Some portion should include discussion on philanthropy, perhaps led by the institution's chief advancement officer and/ or the foundation chief executive.

THE DEVELOPMENT COMMITTEE

In addition to enlisting directors with the capacity and inclination to give and help raise funds, and maintaining the board's focus on the subject, most boards have a committee explicitly charged with providing leadership in this area—usually called the development or fundraising committee.

The majority of foundations reporting to the 2010 AGB survey (72.3 percent) have a standing development committee. Most institution governing boards (82.2 percent) do not, reinforcing the point that foundation boards (where they exist) are the primary fundraising leadership group for most public colleges and universities.

In *Margin of Excellence*, Royster Hedgepeth offers a typical description of the development committee that might be included in a foundation's bylaws:

> *The development committee of the board of directors is responsible for the foundation's comprehensive fundraising program. In carrying out its duties, the committee will set clear expectations and timetables for all phases of fundraising activity and report the results of those efforts to the full board on a quarterly basis. The committee will be chaired by a member of the board of directors and include at least X members of the board. Up to Y additional members may be added to the committee or its subcommittees. The development committee works in concert with the foundation's executive staff and the university's executive leadership to determine fundraising goals, priorities, and timetables.*

Hedgepeth's committee description permits the membership of non-directors on the development committee, a practice that is sometimes followed. But another option often selected in a campaign (discussed further in Chapter 6) is to create a separate campaign-leadership committee with a more diverse membership while retaining the development committee as a more policy-focused standing committee of the board.

I think the name "development committee" is more appropriate than "fundraising committee," although inevitably some board members will casually refer to the committee by the latter term. The distinction is important because fundraising needs to be the responsibility of the entire foundation board, and the term "fundraising committee" might imply that it is not. The development committee is responsible for providing leadership to the board in fundraising, but should not be viewed as the committee that does all the fundraising. Fundraising should be a responsibility of the foundation board as a whole as well as each of its members. It is a too-common misunderstanding that, by creating a development committee, the full board has delegated all responsibility for fundraising to that committee so other members can focus on other areas in which they have particular interest or expertise—for example, investment management of business ventures—reassured that fundraising has been "taken care of."

This may be an issue particularly for a foundation board that is in a process of evolution from a purely fiduciary or advisory body, responsible for the management and investment of gifts, to an active fundraising board. Creation of a development committee may be an initial step in enhancing the board's focus on active fundraising, but if is viewed as an add-on to the board's original role, then the importance of the full board's involvement may not be fully recognized. That may not lead to the full engagement of the board in giving and raising money when all talents and capabilities of every board member need to be employed.

DEVELOPMENT COMMITTEE RESPONSIBILITIES

A job description for the development committee offered by AGB includes the following responsibilities:

- Ensuring that the fundraising program is aligned with the institution's mission and planning priorities as approved by the governing board;
- Encouraging all board members to participate in fundraising programs;
- Identifying prospects and monitoring prospect-solicitation efforts;
- Monitoring the overall development program; and
- Setting goals for board members' giving and soliciting board gifts.

The job description implies a leadership role in establishing fundraising goals and priorities and evaluating the success of fundraising programs. But again, these are activities in which the development committee leads but with which the full board should be concerned. The development committee also may be the originator of policies, such as gift-acceptance policies, that it recommends for acceptance by the full board. In the parlance of the discussion in Chapter 3, these are ownership functions on which the development committee may focus on behalf of the board—and in coordination with the institution.

In *Margin of Excellence*, Hedgepeth states that the development committee should be asking "hard questions" about the fundraising program, which he places in three categories:

Qualitative Questions
1. Does the foundation have a focused, exciting case that supports the institution's mission and aspirations?
2. Has the development committee created a steady flow of donors and an assertive program of engaging them in the life of the institution?
3. Is philanthropy a part of the daily life and culture of the foundation board and the institution? Is the difference philanthropy is making in the quality of the institution and the life of its community visible to the outside observer?
4. Are there effective partnerships between and among the development committee, the foundation board, the foundation staff, the institution's president and executive leadership, and the institutional governing board?
5. Is the development committee leading by example? Is the board following?

Quantitative Questions
1. Has the development committee defined goals for fundraising and a timetable to accomplish them? Is the responsibility for their accomplishment clearly assigned?
2. In conjunction with the foundation staff, has the committee set performance goals for each of the components of the fundraising program?
3. Does the development committee have clear performance guidelines and a schedule of assessment for the committee as a whole and for its individual members?
4. Does the foundation board—led by the development committee—have fundraising goals for which the entire board is responsible? Are those performance goals assessed on a regular basis?
5. Is the board's leadership in terms of giving assessed and reported regularly?

Procedural Questions
1. Does the foundation have a specific plan for selecting, preparing, and assessing members of the development committee?
2. Do development committee members have specific assignments and expectations of performance?
3. Does the committee have a schedule for major gifts solicitations of the size and scope needed for success?
4. Does the committee have a formal gift-acceptance policy? Is it adhered to and reviewed on a regular basis?
5. Does the committee effectively account for fundraising results and engage donors through an active stewardship program?

These are all good questions for the development committee to ask, although it must be emphasized again that many of the answers relate to shared responsibilities of the committee, the full board, the foundation staff, and the institution's board and leadership.

LEADERSHIP IN BOARD GIVING

Although members of the development committee should not be the only people on the foundation board engaged in fundraising, the committee does carry a special responsibility when it comes to ensuring giving from board members. And the development committee's responsibility for board giving goes beyond mere encouragement. Indeed, directors' annual gifts often are solicited by the development committee chair, and if some directors are not meeting their financial obligations, it may fall to the development chair (or the board chair) to discuss the problem with nonparticipants.

The foundation CEO, the institution chief advancement officer, and advancement staff members sometimes solicit board gifts. So do institution presidents. But this can sometimes be awkward; after all, the board is either their employer or at least has significant influence over them in some way. But no such awkwardness should exist among peers, and the solicitation of directors by other directors, especially those who are members of the development committee, often is the most appropriate and effective way to proceed. It brings the power of peer influence and candid discussion to the solicitation conversation.

FUNDRAISING BEYOND THE BOARD

The literature on boards reveals some ambiguity regarding the development committee's role in the actual solicitation of gifts beyond the board itself (that is, with outside prospects). Some suggest that hands-on fundraising should be one of the committee's responsibilities. For example, longtime Lafayette College fundraising executive Gary Evans, in a 2004 AGB "Board Basics" publication about the development committee, wrote the following:

> Members of the development committee are engaged at both ends of the fundraising continuum. At the front end, they set goals, establish policies, and ensure proper attention to institutional priorities. They then delegate to the professional staff the responsibility for preparing the strategies and tactics required to meet those goals and priorities. Committee members—along with **other board members**—return at the end of the process as participants in fulfilling those strategies and tactics designed by professional staff.

As a standing committee of the board, the development committee's primary responsibilities include the planning, policy, and monitoring roles that Evans has identified, plus the responsibility for giving by members of the board. The ambiguity on the question of its role in cultivating and soliciting outside donors may reflect a lack of distinction between the responsibilities of the development committee as a whole and the responsibilities of its members as individual foundation directors. Although individual members of the development committee in their role as directors may be, and indeed should be, active in cultivating and soliciting prospects beyond the board, doing so is not necessarily a responsibility of the development committee per se. Indeed, defining the development committee's role that way may seem to absolve other board members from such participation. Such engagement needs to be a responsibility of the board generally, and of all board members individually.

This distinction is vital: All board members have an obligation to give and to participate actively in fundraising, as they may be able to do so. But solicitation beyond the board itself is not always identified as a responsibility of the development committee as a committee. In part for this reason, most foundations that undertake campaigns create a separate campaign leadership committee in addition to the development committee. Such a committee's activities are focused primarily on raising funds, and this makes it possible to involve foundation directors who are not members of the development committee, as well as other constituents, in the campaign leadership. The subject of campaign leadership committees is discussed further in Chapter 6.

APPOINTMENTS TO THE DEVELOPMENT COMMITTEE

Another question to consider is how foundation directors become members of the development committee. This is part of a larger question that applies to the creation of all board committees, of course. In cases where the board chair permits board members to select their committee assignments or acquiesces to their expressed preferences, chances are good that some of the strongest will end up on the committees concerned with finance and investments—areas in which many members will have expertise and that are perceived to be central to the board's fiduciary responsibility. In such situations, the development committee may not initially attract the board's most effective, affluent, or influential trustees, and its discussions consequently may gravitate toward softer subjects rather than the most important fundraising issues. This is a scenario in which the development committee may wander too far into micromanaging fundraising programs and intrude on the prerogatives of the foundation's CEO or institution's chief advancement officer.

If the development committee is to perform its functions effectively, the board chair must make its importance clear to all board members, actively seek out strong directors to serve on the committee, and emphasize the committee's work in meetings of the full board.

DEVELOPMENT COMMITTEE PITFALLS

The development committee will not succeed if it inadequately addresses its assigned responsibilities. By being aware of three general scenarios, a committee can avoid failure.

The first is the risk of becoming a committee of clappers—that is, a passive committee that receives glowing reports from the foundation or development staff, applauds the success, congratulates the staff, and then retreats into complacency. Especially at foundations where much of the fundraising is conducted by staff members, the foundation CEO or chief advancement officer may see meetings of the development committee as opportunities to present the good news about the professional staff's achievements. Clearly, unless committee members actively set fundraising goals, monitor results, and confront problems in an open and engaged manner, the committee will not meet its responsibilities, and the board will not live up to its obligation as a steward of the foundation in service to the college or university. What's more, a totally passive development committee presents a risky situation for the institution, the institution's president, and the chief advancement officer or foundation chief executive, who should be able to rely on a shared responsibility with the foundation board for fundraising outcomes.

But an opposite extreme scenario is equally destructive: when members of the development committee push the advancement staff to achieve higher goals without accepting their own shared responsibility for fundraising and perhaps without fully understanding the reality of the institution's philanthropic market.

A third dysfunctional scenario is one in which at least some members of the development committee interpret their fundraising role too narrowly. In such a case, members might solicit gifts outside of an organized framework, acting autonomously and perhaps randomly, as they think of possible prospects. Board members should not try to be freelance fundraisers, soliciting prospects outside of a well-coordinated system managed by the development office. That can only lead to confusion and, most likely, to gifts that are smaller than could have been obtained in a coordinated, planned approach. It also is essential that development committee members respect the professional knowledge and judgment of the advancement professionals. They certainly should ask questions and offer suggestions, but they should not impose ideas for new fundraising programs that may be inappropriate to the institution's fundraising strategy or donor constituency.

EVALUATING FOUNDATION BOARDS AND DEVELOPMENT COMMITTEES

What are the characteristics of an effective development committee? In *Margin for Excellence*, Hedgepeth offers the following five attributes, which might be viewed as essential to successful fundraising programs in general:

- Has clearly defined expectations of the committee's fundraising responsibilities and the fundraising performance of its members;

- Establishes measureable outcomes that are evaluated on a regular basis for each set of responsibilities;

- Holds a powerful commitment to succeed, a clear understanding of what constitutes success, and a knowledge of what success means to the life of the institution;

- Holds a focused commitment to raising significant private dollars in support of the institution's mission, needs, and opportunities; and

- Pays unwavering attention to sound fundraising fundamentals, including an active program of donor stewardship that establishes the basis for future fundraising efforts.

How are foundation boards, development committees, and other key players doing, in the judgment of foundation chief executives? In the 2010 AGB survey, foundation CEOs were asked to rate the effectiveness of various bodies, including the development committee (if their foundation has one) in "meeting their responsibilities with regard to the *overall* fundraising program." (A separate question, discussed in Chapter 5, asked about effectiveness on specific fundraising tasks.)

The CEOs' responses are summarized in Table 4.2 and suggest that most foundation boards and development committees are either highly or somewhat effective, but with evident room for improvement. All boards and committees should regularly assess their own performance and that of individual members. Various instruments and methodologies are available for doing so, and the use of an outside consultant is often valuable.

Table 4.2
Foundation CEO Evaluation of Effectiveness in Meeting Responsibilities to the Overall Fundraising Program

(% of foundation CEO responses)

	Highly Effective	Somewhat Effective	Not very effective
The foundation board as a whole	15.6%	60.2%	24.2%
The foundation board executive committee	37.9%	49.2%	12.9%
The development committee of the foundation board	20.2%	55.6%	24.2%
The governing board of the institution	6.7%	30.3%	62.9%

Note to Table 4.2: Percentages refer only to respondents who indicated that the particular body was relevant. For example, some foundations do not have a development committee, and some do not relate to an institutional governing board.

VOICES FROM THE FIELD

Representative comments offered by foundation chief executive officers related to preparing and organizing the board for fundraising:

"We have a brand new development committee, with no formal practice but a willingness to participate, a willingness to learn."

"Our development committee has been in place for two years. It is interested in helping and we are encouraging them in list reviews, identification of prospects, introductions to prospects, and stewardship activities. We do not often involve board members in solicitation calls."

"Right now, our board is more engaged in assessing performance than in helping to achieve results."

"The most important step the board can take to ensure its effectiveness in fundraising is to strengthen the development committee."

"We need to talk about fundraising in our board meetings and particularly in the development committee meetings to have it become part of the culture."

"The most important focus for a foundation chief executive should be the strategic recruitment of board members who have the capacity and propensity for charitable giving."

"At the board meeting, we need to recognize people who engaged in some fundraising action since the previous meeting."

"We have a specific policy on the board's involvement in fundraising. For example, they are required to identify three new prospects every year. And we talk about it at meetings."

"We share reports about who has given."

"We are reorganizing our board. We will move to a 24-member fiduciary board with legal responsibility and a larger development board with responsibility for coordinating fundraising."

Questions for Foundation Boards to Consider

- Are the criteria applied to the selection of new foundation directors appropriate, and do they give adequate weight to the ability and willingness to give and participate in fundraising?

- Are the expectations for giving and fundraising made clear to prospective board members during the enlistment process?

- Are the responsibilities of all directors—both for raising funds and making gifts themselves—regularly discussed at full board meetings?

- Do reports of fundraising results presented to the foundation board include a summary of board giving?

- Are members of the development committee clear about the distinction between their fundraising responsibilities as committee members and their broader responsibilities as individual foundation directors? Do they correctly understand the role of the committee?

CASE STUDY

BUILDING A DEVELOPMENT COMMITTEE:
UNIVERSITY OF IOWA FOUNDATION

Created in 1956, the University of Iowa Foundation is independent of the university and is governed by a 30-member board of directors, which elects its officers and appoints the foundation's president and chief executive officer. It is the preferred channel for private contributions that benefit all areas of the university. The foundation has contributed over $2.2 billion in gifts and commitments to the university from the time of its founding through 2011. Lynette L. Marshall was appointed as the foundation's president in 2006, following a 25-year career at the University of Illinois at Urbana-Champaign.

Prior to Marshall's arrival, the foundation board's standing committees reflected its fiduciary responsibilities, including finance, investment, and audit. Marshall thought it important to have a new committee that would focus on the foundation's fundraising role, and a development committee was created in 2008.

The development committee was established with formal written responsibilities, which include reviewing and advising on fundraising policies; assisting with campaign preparation and volunteer recruitment; leading the board's involvement in identifying, cultivating, and soliciting prospects; engaging in strategic planning; and advising on fundraising priorities, goals, and timetables.

Creation of the development committee has been beneficial in several ways. For example, at each meeting of the full board the development committee chair summarizes gifts and recognizes board members who have provided fundraising leadership, thus keeping fundraising prominent in the minds of foundation directors. The development committee also provides additional opportunities for involvement between full board meetings, especially for directors with expertise related to fundraising, communications, and marketing. Members of the committee also have been instrumental in identifying new prospects and in cultivation—for example, by hosting events in their homes.

Asked what advice she would give to other foundation CEOs creating a new development committee, Marshall offers some key points. She emphasizes that the decision should be carefully considered. While establishing a development committee was the right approach for the University of Iowa Foundation, it may not be the best strategy for every foundation. The foundation's professional staff needs to recognize that having the committee does require more discussion of fundraising strategies. And it is essential to assure that the foundation has a strong staff member who can support the committee and its chair. Marshall also cites the importance of a written job description that clearly spells out the committee's role and responsibilities.

CHAPTER 5

THE FOUNDATION BOARD'S ROLE IN GIVING AND ASKING

F or institutionally related foundations to become successful, active fundraising organizations, boards must go beyond their responsibilities for managing gift funds and accept responsibility—as board members and as individuals—for making personal gifts and becoming engaged in the hands-on work of the foundation's fundraising. In other words, the owners need to join the rest of the team on the field. This responsibility includes their appropriate participation in every phase of the fundraising cycle: identifying prospects, cultivating relationships with donors, soliciting gifts, recognizing donors, and stewarding gifts.

This chapter discusses the involvement of foundation directors in each stage of the fundraising process. As I will discuss in following sections, there are a variety of ways to specify the expectations of foundation directors in giving and fundraising. Figure 5.1 (see page 82) includes a sample of policies that I have excerpted and edited from material available on the Web. Some are quite specific, and others are more broadly stated. There are pros and cons to various approaches.

Figure 5.1

Sample Foundation Policies on Director Expectations and Duties

(Accessed from the Web, March 9, 2011; adapted and excerpted by the author)

Foundation #1—Expectations for Directors

Our expectation is for all members to make [Institution Name] one of their top philanthropic priorities. Major and planned gifts are encouraged, as the primary objective of the [Institution Name] Foundation is to promote and secure private support for the university. Board members also are expected to encourage other individuals and businesses to contribute; however, they are not required to solicit gifts directly. Board members will be invited to sponsor tables or buy tickets to university and foundation events.

Foundation #2—Director Commitment

Contribute—Make a gift of $1,500 during [the fiscal year] to the [foundation name] based on personal interest and ability and make [institution name] a priority in my philanthropic endeavors.

Raise Funds—Participate in the identification, cultivation, solicitation and/or stewardship of donors and prospective donors including peers, corporate contacts, and others.

To agree that if, for any reason, I find myself unable to carry out any of the above duties, I will resign my position as a member of the board, or realize that I may be asked to resign.

Foundation #3—Director Duties

Provide annual, special, and capital support for the university at levels that will inspire others to emulate that support; and

Be available on reasonable demand to work with staff to advance the mission of the foundation by:

a. providing advice and counsel on the general management, operations, and program activities of the foundation;

b. providing or otherwise securing introductions to persons who, by virtue of personal wealth or other resources under their management or control, have potential for new or increased support of the university; and

c. participating in the foundation's efforts to identify, cultivate, and solicit potential donors and in providing stewardship for gifts received.

The sample policies reflect common approaches that will be discussed further in this chapter. One requires a minimum board member gift but explicitly excuses directors from the obligation to solicit gifts from others. Another suggests that the foundation should be a director's highest priority for giving, without specifying any amount. And a third states an expectation that foundation directors give and participate in fundraising at a level commensurate with their abilities. As this chapter will discuss, this sample of policies raises the typical questions and decisions that the foundation board needs to consider.

BOARD MEMBERS AS DONORS

It is well-established in the literature and conventional wisdom that the trustees of independent colleges and universities have an obligation to give and participate in active fundraising for their institutions as an integral part of their overall responsibility as trustees. I once had a conversation with a trustee of George Washington University who challenged that premise. He was a corporate executive who made the point that he did not require or expect that directors of his corporation be stockholders. He argued that the same principle should apply to college and university boards.

I took up the argument, noting that directors of his company were compensated for their service, unlike university boards, so the relationship is inherently different. I also made the case that buying stock in a company is an economic decision, made with the expectation of personal financial gain. Investors can decide whether or not a particular company is a good investment by analyzing its financial results. While stock ownership by insiders may be one criterion that analysts consider in rating a stock, they can use other objective data, such as earnings, in determining an investment decision.

But giving to a college or university is largely an emotional and social decision, driven by complex human motivations, and it is voluntary. There is no obvious bottom line to guide such behavior, and therefore the example set by others who are respected individuals and close to the institution—and thus among the most knowledgeable about it—is an important consideration for many donors. The board makes a statement with its own giving and legitimizes fundraising through its participation. The board's example serves as a substitute for the market; the board's participation validates the cause when there is no financial bottom line to guide investment decisions by others. This trustee eventually yielded to my persuasive logic and became a donor at an appropriate level.

TAKEAWAYS FOR FOUNDATION BOARD MEMBERS

- **Foundation board members should accept the obligation to make financial gifts to the foundation as an inherent part of their responsibility as directors. The board must lead by example and encourage fundraising through its participation.**

- **According to the 2010 AGB survey, more than half of foundations have a formal policy requiring directors to make at least some gift. A little more than a quarter do not specify an amount, and about 30 percent specify a minimum contribution.**

- **Leaders of the board and the institution should cultivate relationships with each foundation director as they would any major donor prospect. They should assess each board member's interests and ability to give.**

- **Board members can advance their foundations' programs not only by making their own gifts, but also by becoming actively involved in the fundraising process, especially in the pursuit of major gifts.**

- **Each and every board member should have a specific fundraising role that is appropriate to his or her own financial means, social position, skills, and talents.**

- **Most foundation directors have achieved great success in professional endeavors, but fundraising requires different skills. Training can help build confidence and a sense of comfort that comes with a familiar experience.**

While many institutionally related foundations in the public sector in the past have been primarily engaged with the receipt and management of gift funds, and some still are, many also are rapidly refocusing their efforts on active fundraising. That will require that foundation board members also accept the obligation to give as a demonstration of their commitment and their confidence in the institution, and as an inherent part of their responsibility as directors.

Board members must lead by example if they are to inspire others to make sacrificial commitments to the institution. The board's example may have an even greater importance as the fundraising environment becomes more competitive and institutions become increasingly reliant on large gifts from a smaller number of donors (that is, as we move toward the narrow portion of the fundraising pyramid shown in Chapter 2).

While public colleges and universities may attract major gifts from corporations and wealthy citizens of the state, region, or community who understand the importance of the institution to the economy and society, the data suggest that most major gift donors are people who have been deeply involved in the college or university, often as a member of a board—whether the governing board of the institution or the board of the foundation. That is demonstrated by many of the major gifts that make the news. For example, in 2011, The Ohio State University received a gift of $100 million from Leslie Wexner, chief executive officer of Limited Brands and chair of the university's board. In the same year, Meyer Luskin, who made his fortune in the animal-feed business and is a member of the board of the UCLA Foundation, gave the foundation $100 million. It was one of the largest gifts that the University of California, Los Angeles had received since a 2002 gift of $200 million from the entertainment entrepreneur David Geffen, after he had served as chair of the university's board of regents, and despite the fact that he is an alumnus of the University of Texas. In other words, it's usually unrealistic to expect major gifts to materialize from strangers, and many are likely to come from sources close to home.

GIVING BY FOUNDATION BOARD MEMBERS

In the 2010 AGB survey, foundation executives were asked what percentage of their directors made various types of gifts within the most recent fiscal year. Their responses indicated that 84.9 percent made an annual gift, 42 percent made a capital gift, and 7.2 percent notified the foundation of a planned gift intention—for example, a bequest provision in their wills. The percentage of board members participating in annual giving is respectable, although 100 percent would be better, of course. A minority were reported as making a capital gift in the fiscal year preceding the survey, but the percentage could vary considerably depending on whether the foundation is currently in the midst of a campaign or not. Planned giving would appear to be an opportunity that foundations might emphasize, given the small percentage of directors that appear to be participating in that way.

The impact of foundation board members varies widely among different types of institutions. In the 2010 AGB survey, foundation executives were asked to provide the total dollars received from foundation directors in the most recent fiscal year. The averages, shown in Table 5.1, demonstrate that giving is highest at foundations associated with research universities, less at master's and baccalaureate institutions, and lowest at two-year institutions (mostly community colleges).

Table 5.1
Average Total of Gifts Received From Foundation Board Members

(most recent fiscal year)

Institution type	Average total
Doctoral-research universities	$4,205,000
Four-year master's institutions	$880,000
Four-year baccalaureate institution	$418,000
Two-year institution	$48,000

Note to Table 5.1: The number of responses to this question from foundations that serve a school or college within a larger university and from system foundations was relatively small. The averages are thus not meaningful and have been excluded.

BOARD GIVING POLICY

As I mentioned previously, some foundations have a formal policy regarding giving by board members. Such policies are often a subject of debate. Table 5.2 summarizes responses to the 2010 AGB survey, indicating that just over one-half (55.4 percent) of foundations have a formal policy requiring that directors make *some* annual gift. But there are two variations. Some require a gift but do not specify an amount (25.7 percent), and others state a specific minimum annual gift for foundation directors (29.7 percent). Another 36.6 percent of foundations have an informal expectation that board members make an annual gift, and 7.9 percent solicit board members but have no policy guiding their responses. No foundation reported that board members are not asked to give.

Table 5.2

Expectations for Board Giving

	2010 AGB survey (foundations)
There is a formal policy that requires a minimum annual gift.	29.7%
There is a formal policy that all board members should give but no minimum amount is specified.	25.7%
There is an informal expectation that all board members should give but no formal policy.	36.6%
All board members are solicited, but there is no specific expectation or requirement.	7.9%

For those foundations that do have a minimum-gift policy, the required amount varies widely, as shown in Table 5.3. The most common range is between $1,000 and $4,999. The overall average is just under $2,000. Again, data from AGB's 2004 survey of *independent* college and university trustees is also shown in Table 5.3 for comparison. The comparison suggests that independent-institution trustees have somewhat higher expectations for giving. But it must be emphasized that the independent-sector data is several years old, and policies may have changed in the meantime.

Table 5.3

Level of Minimum Gift Required

(Percentage of foundations/independent institutions that have minimum annual giving requirements)

Range	% of foundation responses (2010)	% of independent institution responses (2004)
$25,000+	0.0%	0.0%
$10,000-$24,000	5.0%	27.5%
$5,000-$9,999	13.0%	34.5%
$1,000-$4,999	82.0%	24.1%
< $1,000	0.0%	13.7%

The chief executives of foundations that do not have a minimum giving requirement for their boards hold mixed views on the subject. When asked if they would favor one, a slight majority (51.3 percent) said that they would not, while 48.7 percent said that they would favor such a policy.

The idea of setting a minimum board giving requirement has its pros and cons, as well as its admirers and detractors. "Establishing minimum benchmarks for board members' giving," wrote AGB's Richard D. Legon in a 2001 *Trusteeship* article, "can be the most challenging and controversial part of a policy statement on philanthropy." On the positive side, such a policy makes the board's financial obligation explicit, increases the likelihood that every board member will give, simplifies the response to prospective directors' questions about what is expected, and makes it possible to project future board support. On the negative side, it is not always simple to determine what the minimum should be, and there may be risks in setting a minimum that works for all members of the board.

All good boards seek diversity in their membership, based not only on considerations of gender, ethnicity, and other demographic characteristics, but also in terms of professional skills, representation of important constituencies, and other variables. It may be that the board needs the views and expertise of some whose capacities to give may be limited. Although the practice has admirers and critics, some boards even include student and faculty representation. (That debate is beyond the scope of this discussion.) If the minimum gift is set low enough to be within reach for all members of a diverse board—say, less than $1,000—the floor risks becoming a ceiling, and board members with the ability to make much larger gifts may decide merely to meet this minimum requirement. That could result in the institution receiving less revenue than if everyone gave in proportion to his or her financial means.

Of course, it also is possible to set the minimum gift higher—say, $5,000 or more—and make exceptions for those who are unable to meet this financial expectation. That option, however, could embarrass those who are the subject of the exception. It runs the risk of having a board composed of first-class and second-class members—those who give the minimum and those who do not—and that the former will dominate, while the latter defer, in board decisions.

Some suggest setting the standard for giving in terms of a percentage of personal income and wealth—for example, an annual gift equivalent to 2 percent of personal annual income within three years and a campaign commitment equivalent to a minimum of 2.5 percent of net worth. That may seem fair, and it does require more of those who are affluent than of those who are less so. It also has the advantage of not requiring exceptions to be made; even a young alumnus should be able to give something to the annual fund over three years. But setting such a standard still invites the risk that the floor becomes a ceiling and that some board members thus give less than they are able. It also may strike some foundation directors as just slightly intrusive. If we assume that every trustee is following the rule, then we would be able to know their income and net worth from the size of his or her gift.

Finally, setting a minimum standard for annual giving does not take into account a person's other financial or family obligations. For example, it is common for entrepreneurs to acquire their wealth in windfalls when companies go public or are sold. Given the risks they face, some are reluctant to make commitments that extend into the future and do not have the liquidity to make substantial annual gifts. Relationships with such people are well worth developing and sustaining, however, because they may make sizable gifts once their circumstances permit. In other words, entrepreneurs may be episodic donors, who give in big chunks when they receive an inflow of new wealth from a business transaction, rather than regular annual donors with predictable income levels and increases in wealth. Too much emphasis on annual giving, the timing of gifts, or formulas for giving may not be a good fit with the realities of such donors' financial lives.

Indeed, I once worked with a board member who was in just that situation. Although I emphasized that even a token annual gift of $1,000 or so would help to achieve the goal of 100-percent board participation—and he made one for that reason—he also often seemed resentful at being asked. My impression was that he found the solicitation for a token gift to be almost an insult and so little as to be inconsequential—a waste of time for him and for me. He always said that "I will give it when I get it" and referred to his eventual plans to sell his company. Eventually, he sold the company and kept his word with a major gift. Although I thought the annual gift was essential, my asking always seemed like an annoyance to him, and I worried that my insistence on it might erode my excellent relationship with him over the long haul. Fortunately, it did not, and the long haul turned out to be rewarding.

Some suggest that a board member's gift should be at least as large as he or she makes to any other nonprofit organization. In other words, the foundation should at least share the top spot on its directors' lists of favored causes. Some broaden this to say that the foundation should be among the board member's top two or three highest priorities for giving. Others propose the reasonable, but somewhat vague, standard that every board member's gift should represent a stretch for that person that goes beyond his or her usual giving limits. But both of these standards are open to interpretation and difficult to enforce.

Another approach is simply to say that every member of the board is expected to make some annual gift appropriate to his or her ability and to respond to campaigns with special gifts—again, according to financial ability and consistent with each person's interests. Each trustee is then cultivated and solicited in the same way as any major gift prospect. They are presented with a specific ask appropriate to his or her known financial ability, motivations, and interests.

That approach may lead to disappointment, however, if a director who accepts election to the board does not give as expected (although the decision may be remembered when the director's term expires and the question of re-election comes before the board). The risk of such disappointments may be balanced by the likelihood that an individualized approach to solicitation will yield more revenue in the long run than will setting one uniform standard for board giving.

In my opinion, and despite its Marxist overtones, "from each according to his or her ability" is a standard with which most will agree when it comes to giving. The responsibility of development professionals and board leaders is to know what each director's ability really is and to develop relationships with board members that permit candid conversations along those lines. That requires a careful assessment of each board member's interests and capabilities and the investment of time and effort to take a personalized approach. It is often the board chair, the chair of the development committee, or another board officer who needs to have the conversations with board colleagues about their gifts. That is perhaps a more demanding and less comfortable approach than setting a simple standard requirement, but it is likely to be effective.

Like the majority of foundation CEOs who participated in the 2010 AGB survey, I am at best ambivalent about the usefulness of setting specific minimum annual gift requirements for individual board members. Philanthropic giving is by nature voluntary, and thus compulsory giving is in essence an oxymoron. A person's decision to give at the full level of his or her capacity is based primarily not on rational analysis but on feeling. As Harold J. Seymour reminds us in his classic 1966 book *Designs for Fundraising* (second edition: the Fundraising Institute, 1988), "The heart has to prompt the mind to go where logic points the way." The feeling that motivates exceptional giving develops slowly, as a person's relationship with an institution and with others who are associated with the institution deepens over time. As in romance, it is not wise or even possible to dictate or try to rush what can only grow at its own pace.

That is why major gifts to colleges and universities usually follow a long period of cultivation in which a person's relationship with the institution is nurtured through communication and involvement. We should assume that foundation directors will be motivated to make gifts in the same way as other people. Service on the board is the highest and most intense level of involvement for any volunteer, and the experience is likely to elicit a desire to give at a meaningful level. Seymour also suggests that people naturally tend to resist instruction on their "obligations." When told what they "must" do, most people will respond by doing what is demanded, but not much more.

As I wrote previously, others may disagree, and I certainly allow for the possibility that they may be right. The approach that I've described may sound "soft" to some people, especially to those who come from a business background and are accustomed to hard negotiation. But in my experience, it is a pragmatic strategy that yields results, if properly and consistently applied.

One point is clear: Foundation directors have an obligation to support the foundation as much as they can. They incur that obligation in exchange for the privilege of serving in such an important position—a role on which the future of public higher education may well depend. Most board members will understand that. Those who fail to meet their obligations should not be left un-reminded. Leaders of the board and the institution should cultivate relationships with each foundation director as they would any major donor prospect. If done properly, that should minimize the need for reminding.

BOARD MEMBERS AS FUNDRAISERS

As stated earlier, board members can advance their foundation's program not only by making their own gifts but by becoming actively involved in the fundraising process, especially in the pursuit of major gifts. The process of major gifts fundraising is depicted in Figure 5.1 and includes five essential steps: identifying prospects, cultivating relationships with prospects, soliciting major gift prospects, acknowledging and recognizing donors, and stewarding both the gift and the relationship on an ongoing basis. The process is sometimes depicted as a cycle, in which stewardship blends into cultivation of the donor in preparation for soliciting the next gift. As discussed in the following sections, foundation directors can play an essential role in each stage.

Figure 5.1
The Major Gift Fundraising Process

Identify and qualify prospects → Cultivate relationships → Solicit the gift → Acknowledge the gift and recognize the donor → Steward the gift and the relationship

Identification of Prospects

Most development offices have skilled staff members who work in the area of prospect research. Such professionals continuously analyze the lists of the institution's constituents to determine who has the financial capacity to become major donors and whose history suggests some level of interest—perhaps previous giving to the institution, involvement as members of the alumni association or on another board or committee, or a history of giving to other organizations that suggests a philanthropic nature.

In addition, foundation board members may have information that is not available through the usual public sources used by prospect researchers. Board members may know of an individual's wealth in areas that are not revealed by public data. In particular, they may be able to evaluate a prospect's potential interest, perhaps discovering through a conversation that he or she would be receptive to cultivation by the foundation. Most important, members of the foundation board may know the prospect or others who have a relationship with the prospect, and that can point the way to a conversation about the college or university.

While the usual prospect-research resources may identify connections between individuals—for example, common membership on other boards or membership in the same club—determining the actual relationship between them is best accomplished by speaking directly with others who know them. As the foundation's eyes and ears in the broad community, board members may be a primary source of such insight. However, foundation chief executives who responded to the 2010 AGB survey indicated that only 31.6 percent of foundation directors had identified a new prospect within the past year.

Cultivation and Solicitation of Prospects

Board members' responsibility for philanthropy extends beyond their own personal support to active involvement in the cultivation and solicitation of donors to the foundation. That point is clear in every statement about the board's fundraising role. But it does not address from whom the board should solicit gifts or how that activity should fit within a coordinated development program.

Board members have the relationships, credibility, and stature to communicate the importance of an institution's cause in a way that the foundation CEO, other development or foundation staff, and even the president of the institution cannot. Although today's fundraising programs include more direct interaction between advancement staff and major donors, the involvement of at least some board members in the cultivation and solicitation of major donors can be vital, especially for the top prospects from whom the largest gifts are anticipated. This reflects simple human nature. As Seymour said many years ago, among the most powerful of human motivations is pride of association, the desire to be "a worthwhile member of a worthwhile group." Because foundation board members are in positions of leadership at their respected institutions and are usually prominent citizens in their states, communities, professions, and industries, their solicitation of someone for a major gift is in effect inviting that person to join the inner circles and to take a place among the elite. It is an invitation that carries greater psychological power than a solicitation delivered by a fundraising professional or even by the president of the college or university.

The importance of the peer relationship in solicitation is illustrated by an experience I had when, as vice president for development and alumni affairs, I accompanied a board member on a memorable major gift visit. The board member was a prominent real-estate developer, unquestionably one of the leading figures in his industry and a highly respected, active member of the local business community. The prospect also happened to be a real-estate developer, and it was apparent from the moment that he greeted the trustee and me at his office door that he was flattered by this board member's visit.

After some small talk, our board member asked me to summarize the goals of the university's campaign. The prospect listened politely, but as soon as I finished my presentation, he turned immediately to the board member and steered the discussion toward recent developments in the local real-estate market, seemingly uninterested in the university's plans. This peer talk went on for awhile, until eventually the prospect returned to the subject of the university. "Mike," he said to me, "I appreciate what you have said. You make a persuasive argument, you do your job well, and I do intend to support the campaign. But," he said, turning to the board member, "Bob [not his real name], I am especially impressed with what you are doing for the university. I know how busy you are, and I am truly flattered that you have taken the time from your schedule to come and see me today. This must be important to you and, if that's the case, then it deserves my careful attention. I had planned to make a more modest gift to this campaign, but after your visit here today, I want to help you be successful in this project. So I am going to talk to my wife and see if we can find a way to match what you have done with your own gift."

A vice president visiting alone would have come away with a gift to the campaign, no doubt. But in this prospect's mind, I was simply "doing my job." He may have thought I was doing it well, but it was not my professionalism that caused him to reconsider his gift. It was the authenticity and credibility added by the presence of a prominent volunteer and the example of that board member's own commitment. The power of a peer relationship tipped the scale. For me, this experience offered a classic example of the power of board leadership in fundraising.

In the 2010 AGB survey, foundation executives were asked what percentage of their board members had participated in solicitation activities during the most recent year. Their responses indicate that 30 percent had been responsible for obtaining a gift from a corporation or private foundation, 14.2 percent had participated in a solicitation together with the institution president or an advancement professional, and 8.3 percent had undertaken a solicitation alone. This suggests that while most foundation board members may make their own gifts, fewer take the next step to become solicitors of gifts from others.

GIVING AND GETTING

A companion to the board minimum-gift argument is the "give-or-get" debate. Some experts advocate setting an amount that every board member is expected either to give personally or raise from others in a year or in the course of a year or a campaign. The pros and cons of give-or-get are similar to those of requiring minimum personal gifts from board members. That is, not every member of the board may have equal influence to raise significant amounts from others; indeed, that ability—like personal wealth and income—is almost certain to be unequally distributed among board members.

Moreover, the give-or-get requirement raises potential problems for the development staff. Its members must figure out how best to manage prospects, with a cultivation and solicitation plan for each that is custom-designed and ideally matches prospect with solicitor. For example, two or three board members may know many of the same prospects in a community or have contacts at a major local company. Development professionals must be able to determine which of them should be part of the team that solicits a gift from each prospect. To return to the football-team metaphor, the chief advancement officer as quarterback, in consultation with the coach, must decide who will run the ball.

Individual board members under a mandate to give or get a prescribed amount could become competitive for the same prospects, perhaps placing the development staff in an awkward situation and creating a mismatch of solicitor and prospect that will produce less than maximum results. It also might tempt a board member who lacks the appropriate skills to act as a solicitor, when a better fundraising role might be in the areas of donor cultivation and stewardship.

It is usually unrealistic to expect most board members to be able to tap new sources of support currently unrelated to the college or university, although it does happen. A well-connected member of the board may be able to attract gifts from social or business associates who are not within the institution's usual constituency, especially if they have an understanding of the impact that the college or university has on the state or community, possibly with positive implications for their own businesses. Such opportunities may be generally greater for public rather than independent colleges and universities, since public institutions may be viewed as important resources of benefit to all citizens. But in most cases, gifts from people with no affiliation are relatively modest, and when they do occur, they are often not repeated on a regular basis. Prospects for major gifts are most likely to be individuals with an existing link to the college or university, and thus are well-known to more than one person in the institution's community.

In addition, it is not always easy to determine who actually secured the gift and, thus, to whose fundraising total the gift should be credited. This is analogous to the issue of measuring the performance of the development staff. Often, many people are engaged in the relationship with a prospective donor, and the one who actually solicits the gift may indeed have made the least contribution to preparing the prospect for a positive response. Assigning credit for a gift to one individual solicitor, whether that person is a development officer or a board member, may create a competitive environment that leads to squabbles over who is assigned the most-promising prospects and who did the most important work. Such an atmosphere detracts from teamwork and the time spent actually raising funds.

An alternative approach to setting a minimum give-or-get target is to define a specific fundraising role for each board member that is appropriate to his or her own financial means, social position, skills, and talents. That may involve participating in prospect-cultivation events, or opening the door to a foundation or corporation for a visit by the president or a member of the advancement staff. It may mean accompanying the president, foundation CEO, or chief advancement officer on a prospect visit, or it may mean accepting primary responsibility for cultivating and soliciting specific prospects. In any case, every board member's involvement in cultivation and solicitation should be part of an overall plan coordinated by the development office and not a reaction to an arbitrary requirement to give or get. In the context of a board that has been well prepared to understand and accept its fundraising responsibility, it should be assumed that every director will respond enthusiastically when asked to perform an appropriate role.

SOLICITATION STRATEGIES

How many people should be a part of a gift solicitation team, and who should they be? A powerful combination includes a board member accompanied by a member of the institution's administrative leadership—the president, the chief advancement officer, or perhaps a dean or director of a program that is the particular focus of a solicitation. The board member brings the credibility and power, while the institutional representative brings the in-depth knowledge of the institution's programs and plans and the ability to respond to specific questions.

Such a team can influence both the prospect's heart and head in a way that individual team members alone may be unprepared to accomplish. Board member visits with prospects and donors should be followed up with a debriefing and a written report entered into the advancement office's records. Including the president or an advancement officer in such visits may ease the completion of such necessary tasks and ensure that the history of the conversation is thoroughly and accurately recorded.

Most foundation board members are highly successful and confident people who have achieved great success in their own business and professional endeavors. But fundraising requires different skills, and not every director can be confident that his or her skills will translate successfully into this arena. Training can help build confidence and a sense of comfort that comes with a familiar experience. In addition to whatever new skills such training may provide, the exercise can also help keep the focus on fundraising and reinforces awareness of the board's fundraising responsibilities.

STEWARDSHIP

Today's fundraising literature increasingly emphasizes the importance of ongoing stewardship. Indeed, many development offices have added special staff to improve and intensify communication with existing donors concerning the long-term use and impact of their gifts. For the fundraising staff, stewardship in practice means continuing systematic cultivation of donors, who remain prospects for future gifts.

For foundation directors, the concept of stewardship has a double meaning. Their personal involvement in maintaining relationships with donors is important, because it conveys recognition and gratitude from the highest level of the foundation's leadership. And their fiduciary responsibility requires board members to ensure that donors' gifts actually are managed according to their wishes and used to maximum effect in pursuing the institution's mission and goals.

In the 2010 AGB survey, foundation CEOs reported that 60.6 percent of foundation directors had participated in an event or other activity related to recognition or stewardship of a donor. That is much higher than the percentage who participated in solicitations. It may be that stewardship is a more comfortable activity than solicitation for many board members, and engaging them in this aspect of the process may be a good way to get started with those who are new to fundraising.

When the process of involving volunteers in fundraising is just beginning, it is essential to provide those volunteers with opportunities for early success, to build their comfort level with the entire endeavor. Cultivation activities may be an easy way for some board members to begin interacting with donors in a comfortable way. And when volunteers are assigned to solicitations, it is wise to ensure that the early visits are likely to be positive encounters with a positive result. After a few successes, many volunteers will develop an enthusiasm that might have been difficult to predict, gradually taking on more challenging assignments. Eventually they will experience a failure, but by then they will have been bolstered by successes and are likely to persevere.

EVALUATING FOUNDATION BOARDS' PERFORMANCE

How effective are foundation boards in fulfilling their responsibilities as active participants in fundraising? As summarized in Table 5.4, the overwhelming majority are viewed by the chief executives as either highly or somewhat effective on a variety of activities that relate directly to their roles as donors and fundraisers. Only a relatively small percentage is "highly effective" on some crucial points: introducing new prospects (9 percent), holding board members accountable (9 percent), and participating in solicitations (10 percent). The majority response on all points is "somewhat effective," so there is room for improvement.

It must be acknowledged that the question allows for some ambiguity. Other data from the 2010 AGB survey suggest that the percentage of foundation directors involved in some aspects of fundraising is not high. And yet the foundation executive officers rated their directors' performance as at least "somewhat effective" on some activities, such as identifying prospects and soliciting gifts, in which a minority seem to be engaged. Perhaps the best way to think about the data in Table 5.4 is to say that *when* foundation board members participate in fundraising, they tend to be somewhat or even highly effective. That should encourage board members and reassure them that they can make a valuable contribution in this area.

Table 5.4
Effectiveness of the Foundation Board In Fundraising Activities

(Percentage of CEO responses)

	Highly effective	Somewhat effective	Not very effective
Understanding the foundation's fundraising/development strategy	24.0%	59.0%	17.0%
Understanding the foundation's mix of contributions (e.g., annual giving, planned giving, individuals, corporations, private foundations, etc.)	28.0%	55.0%	17.0%
Introducing the institution/foundation to new prospects	9.0%	58.0%	33.0%
Making personal financial contributions	33.0%	58.0%	9.0%
Participating in fundraising activities and solicitations	10.0%	66.0%	24.0%
Holding board members accountable for fulfilling their fundraising responsibilities	9.0%	53.0%	38.0%

VOICES FROM THE FIELD

Representative comments offered by foundation chief executive officers regarding the foundation board in giving and fundraising:

"Our board members know that fundraising is their primary responsibility and are improving in this area after completing a successful major gifts campaign."

"Currently our foundation board does not play a significant role in fundraising. Just this past year they have engaged in a feasibility study and board development plan to begin a more active fundraising role."

"Our foundation board members make their own major gifts and join with the foundation and institution CEOs and staff in making solicitations and in the stewardship of donors."

"The most important step the board can take is to develop a self-assessment tool that includes activities associated with the fundraising process."

"The foundation board should introduce new prospects to the president and the foundation executive director."

"Board members should make their own annual gifts and special campaign gifts before asking, and exercise proper stewardship of gifts received, to demonstrate a commitment to their fiduciary responsibility."

"The foundation CEO needs to find one or two board members who can be used as examples and recognize them for taking part in asking."

"Ask foundation board members to undertake a specific fundraising task—set up a lunch, attend an event, etc."

"Our board members are very committed as donors themselves but are not as active as we would like in helping to build and advance relationships with new prospective donors."

"Our board is in transition from a grantmaking to a fundraising body."

Questions for Foundation Boards to Consider

- Has the foundation board discussed and agreed upon an approach to director giving?
- Does this approach require all directors to make gifts of a specific level? Is such a policy desirable or undesirable for your board?
- Do all board members understand the policy?
- Do board leaders and advancement or foundation staff regularly talk with foundation board members about their giving in one-on-one conversations?
- Do foundation directors participate in the identification, cultivation, and solicitation of donor prospects? If so, how often?
- Does the foundation CEO or development staff seek and support the board's participation in these activities?
- What is the typical format of major gift solicitations? Who usually makes the visit, and who determines the composition of the team?

CASE STUDY

ENGAGING THE BOARD IN FUNDRAISING:
RAMAPO COLLEGE FOUNDATION

Ramapo College, founded in 1969 in Mahwah, N.J., is a four-year, public liberal arts college with 6,008 students. The college is governed by a board of trustees appointed by the governor of the state. The Ramapo College Foundation is the college's fundraising arm and has a board of 58 members who serve three-year terms. Cathleen Davey, the college's vice president for institutional advancement and the foundation's executive director, has been at Ramapo since 1992, following a 10-year career at Seton Hall University.

The Ramapo College Foundation has clear policies regarding the involvement of its board in giving and fundraising. Every member is expected to provide an annual gift and to make Ramapo one of their top-three philanthropic priorities. Some board members are corporate officers and help to secure corporate gifts and sponsorships, but they also make personal annual gifts.

In addition to personal giving, board members are expected to identify between three and five new prospects each year and introduce the college president or vice president to those prospects. The definition of "prospect" is broad. The individuals might include potential donors as well as employers who can provide student internships, possible guest speakers, and candidates for service on advisory councils at the college. Some board members also make introductions to leaders in their own industries, new business people moving into the college's area, and other organizations that may become partners with the college.

The board's involvement is coordinated by the foundation staff. As Davey notes, engaging a board of 58 people is a "full-time job." A vice chair of the foundation board works closely with the foundation staff to identify ways that each board member can help in cultivating new friends. Opportunities may include dinners with the president, campus visits, performing-arts events on campus, and other settings. At every meeting, the board chair recognizes members who have participated in prospect introductions and other fundraising activities, to provide encouraging examples.

Davey emphasizes the importance of knowing each member of the foundation board and identifying the right type of involvement for each individual. "Prepare them and ensure that they are successful," she advises. "When people have a good experience, they want to do more."

CHAPTER 6

THE FOUNDATION BOARD IN A CAMPAIGN

Before the early 20th century, higher education fundraising—then almost entirely an activity of independent colleges and universities—was generally not organized. It was conducted by presidents and perhaps a few trustees, and it was episodic—usually undertaken to meet a specific need, such as a new building. The concept of an intensive campaign was developed in the first decade of the last century by YMCA fundraisers and was introduced to higher education by fundraising consultants, who managed many of the early campaigns.

For most of the 20th century, it was most common for higher education institutions to undertake periodic capital campaigns, usually to raise funds for a specific new facility. Annual giving and planned giving initiatives either were suspended during the major campaign or continued alongside the campaign as distinct programs. In the traditional capital campaign, most gifts were either paid outright or pledged over a relatively short period, typically three to five years, consistent with the construction of the new building that most campaigns supported.

COMPREHENSIVE CAMPAIGNS

Today, most college and university campaigns are comprehensive campaigns. Their overall goals include not only funds for bricks-and-mortar projects and endowment gifts, but also annual giving and other gifts for support of current programs over the campaign period. Planned gifts, which are often intended to meet endowment goals, also are part of comprehensive campaigns.

Most campaigns are institution-wide. At large universities, for example, they usually include university wide priorities as well as specific goals and objectives related to the various academic units, all under one umbrella with an overarching goal and theme. While colleges and universities still undertake focused or special-purpose campaigns, the comprehensive campaign model has become the norm, in both independent and public institutions. The campaign's comprehensive nature accounts in part for the large goals that many announce; the goal usually includes all gifts for all purposes received by the institution or the foundation during the defined period of the campaign.

The campaign has essential defining characteristics, which distinguish it from ordinary, ongoing fundraising. They include:

• an announced goal and deadline;

• specific objectives or priorities based on institutional strategic planning;

• organized volunteer leadership, including a prominent chair or co-chairs and a strong leadership committee;

• rated prospect lists with a plan to solicit gifts "from the top down and the inside out";

• a campaign plan that includes defined phases, unfolding over a period of years; and

• high visibility intended to gain the attention of the full constituency and maintain the urgency of reaching the public goal by the announced deadline.

Progress toward the campaign goal is measured in commitments, which may encompass outright gifts, pledges, and planned gift arrangements created during the campaign, although the latter may not be realized for years. As a result, managers of comprehensive campaigns need to communicate clearly the purposes of the campaign and how commitments are credited toward the goal, lest there be a misperception among faculty members (and perhaps even board members) that a large amount of unrestricted money will be available for allocation at the end of the campaign. The campaign total represents the sum of several different categories of current and future revenues, and often relatively little is available for discretionary use at the campaign's conclusion. Indeed, to the extent that unrestricted gifts are included in the campaign total, they are likely to be gifts to the annual fund during the years of the campaign, which usually have been expended in the year they were received to support current operating needs.

A campaign represents the institution's and the foundation's all-out commitment to fundraising and is among its most visible initiatives. The term "campaign" (and much of the vocabulary associated with it) has military connotations; indeed, some top advancement professionals have compared such efforts as something akin to war—albeit with the goal of building an institution rather than destroying an enemy. A campaign's intensity, its all-out focus on victory, and the unthinkable nature of failure complete the metaphor. (Of course, most campaigns include a "kickoff," a term drawn from football!)

During a campaign, the president may spend as much as one-half of his or her time in activities related to fundraising. The staff usually will be "eating, sleeping, and breathing" the campaign, especially during the most intense phases. And the board must mobilize its energies and resources at a maximum level.

TAKEAWAYS FOR FOUNDATION BOARD MEMBERS

- Many colleges and universities today will find themselves either planning a campaign, engaged in one, or just completing one.

- Today most campaigns are comprehensive: Their goals include not only funds for facilities and endowments, but also annual giving and other gifts for support of current programs.

- Even before planning begins, it is important to assess if the institution and foundation are ready to undertake a campaign. The foundation board should be engaged in the planning process in appropriate ways and understand the campaign's goals, objectives, and policies.

- A campaign cannot succeed unless the board collectively produces an adequate portion of the overall goal through its own gifts. The amount board members should give depends on the size and scope of the institution's constituency and the types of gifts the campaign will encompass.

- The foundation board's universal participation in the nucleus fund is essential in campaigns. Foundation directors are likely to be among the leadership donors whose commitments set the tone for all other donors.

- A comprehensive campaign is also a communications strategy for the institution. Achieving the goal is a victory worthy of visible and enthusiastic celebration. Success breeds success.

Campaign goals became a topic of debate in the 1990s, with some critics saying that goals were losing credibility because they were too large and all-encompassing. Critics also pointed to inconsistency among institutions in the length of campaigns and accounting rules applied to crediting commitments toward the goal, which made it difficult for board members and others to compare them. The Council for Advancement and Support of Education (CASE) responded by developing campaign-reporting standards intended to bring more uniformity to the length and accounting rules for campaigns, providing a greater ability to compare them across institutions. The CASE guidelines have been revised as campaign practices have evolved, most recently in 2008. It is important for board members to understand that campaign accounting may not follow the same rules as the foundation's financial statements. The purpose of campaign reports is to show progress toward the goal, which is often measured in commitments of various types that are not reflected on the foundation's balance sheet. However, there need to be clear policies on how gifts are credited toward the campaign goal and the ability to reconcile campaign reports with financial reports using both sets of applicable rules.

Many colleges and universities today will find themselves either planning a campaign, engaged in one, or just completing one. Even in that last period, preliminary thinking about the next campaign will most likely begin shortly after the victory celebration. The interval between campaigns has become increasingly brief, and some colleges and universities are in virtually continuous campaigns, constantly maintaining a high level of fundraising intensity. However, it was widely reported in the news media that some institutions delayed announcing campaigns in the 2008-10 period, awaiting a return to more favorable economic conditions.

In the 2010 AGB survey, the majority of foundation CEOs indicated that they were currently engaged in the public phase of a campaign or had completed a campaign within the most recent five years; 35.8 percent were in the public phase, and 18.9 percent had completed a campaign within the most recent five years. For simplicity, in this chapter both groups are simply referred to as being "in a campaign." Because several survey questions related specifically to results in the quiet period of the campaign, only institutions that were "in a campaign" were asked to respond to additional campaign-related questions. In other words, those currently in the quiet phase were not included.

The average campaign goal was varied by institution type, as presented in Table 6.1. (The table also includes data on the nucleus fund, which will be discussed later in this chapter.) The closing date of campaigns ranged from 2006 (for completed campaigns) to 2020 (for those currently underway). Most campaigns had been completed in 2010 or were scheduled to conclude in 2011.

Table 6.1
Average Campaign Goals and Nucleus-Fund Totals

Institution type	Average campaign goal	Average amount raised in the nucleus fund	Nucleus fund as percentage of campaign goal
Research/doctoral institutions	$426 million	$220 million	52.0%
Four-year master's institutions	$48 million	$25 million	52.0%
Four-year baccalaureate institutions	$35 million	$19 million	54.0%
Two-year institutions	$9 million	$4 million	44.0%

Note to Table 6.1: One foundation responding to this question supports a single academic unit within an institution and was in a campaign with a goal of $150 million. No foundations supporting a multicampus system reported being in a campaign.

PROCEEDING IN PHASES

Successful campaigns follow a well-established process, unfolding in phases over a period of years. The CASE guidelines recommend that campaigns be no longer than eight years, including a quiet period, or silent phase, and a public phase that follows formal announcement. Figure 6.1 depicts the phases of a typical campaign as they are commonly defined. Some people may describe the phases of a campaign using different terms, but the activities that they describe are similar, and there is general agreement on the model. The following sections discuss the involvement of the foundation board in each of these phases.

Figure 6.1

Phases of the Campaign

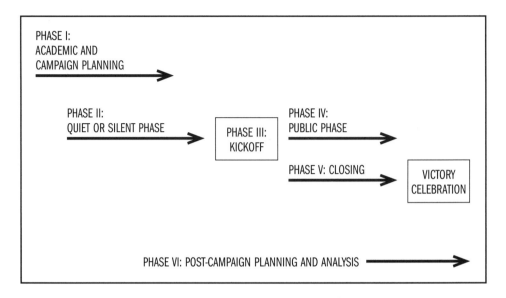

Some board members feel frustrated by the long process of planning and preparation as well as by the quiet phase of solicitation that precedes public announcement of the campaign. They may want to just get on with things, announce the goal, and begin broad solicitations of the entire constituency. It's important to resist this temptation, however. In campaign fundraising, adhering to the process is essential to building consensus and support that ultimately will lead to achieving the dollar goal and the specific objectives that the campaign is intended to serve.

While fundraising is a blend of art and science, a campaign includes a significant amount of the latter, based on about a century of evidence from fundraising efforts in the United States. It is vital that a campaign unfold according to established principles lest it be doomed to failure at the outset.

ASSESSING CAMPAIGN READINESS

Even before planning begins—sometimes years before—it is important to assess if the institution and the foundation are ready to undertake a campaign. Such an assessment may identify areas of weakness in which efforts need to be undertaken, sometimes requiring months or longer to complete, in order to prepare the resources and conditions essential to campaign success.

A number of authors have suggested criteria for assessing readiness—in other words, prerequisites for campaign success. Some checklists produce a numerical readiness score. But many situations are complex, and a single total score may obscure the finer points. A preliminary readiness assessment may be most useful as a vehicle for identifying relative strengths and weaknesses and the work that needs to be done to prepare for a campaign—that is, as a guide to planning rather than as a standard by which to make a go/no-go decision.

The following criteria are similar to those articulated by various other authors and describe conditions that define ideal circumstances under which a college or university embarks upon a campaign:

- The institution has a clear vision of its mission, its place in higher education, and distinct qualities that set it apart from others in terms of its impact on society. That is, it has a strong case for support.

- The institution has a plan for its future growth and improvement that is based on academic priorities.

- Specific fundraising goals and objectives have been identified and are rooted in the institution's strategic priorities, as articulated in the plan.

- Major objectives of the proposed campaign are well understood internally and enjoy a broad consensus among foundation directors, the institution's governing board members, campus leaders, faculty and staff members, and other stakeholders at various levels.

- Members of the foundation board and the institution's board are committed to the institution's plan and the goals of the campaign. They are prepared to support the campaign with time, energy, and personal resources, commensurate with their ability.

- The institution's president is well regarded, willing to commit sufficient time to the campaign, and is able to articulate the importance of the campaign's priorities.

- Other administrative leaders of the institution—for example, deans and program directors—are supportive of the campaign and willing to play appropriate roles, including participation in the cultivation and solicitation of prospects with interest in their units or activities.

- The institution has identified potential volunteer leaders of the campaign who are committed to its purposes, well-known and respected in its constituency, prepared to commit sufficient time to leading the campaign, and, preferably, have experience in fundraising.

- There are prospects who have the capacity to make leadership gifts totaling a significant portion of the anticipated campaign goal—that is, for the nucleus fund— and who have been cultivated to a point of readiness to make such commitments.

- A sufficient number of prospects have connections to the institution, a known or demonstrated commitment to its purposes, and the financial capacity to provide the gifts required to attain the balance of the proposed goal.

- The institution or foundation has adequate knowledge (including records, prospect research, and other information) regarding the interests, philanthropic priorities, and life and financial circumstances of its prospects to formulate solicitation strategies that will be timely and appropriate.

- The advancement office or foundation is led by a fundraising professional who is well regarded by the board, has access to the president and other senior leaders of the institution, and preferably has significant campaign experience.

- The development and foundation staffs are sufficient in size, are properly configured, and possess the experience and skills to execute a campaign.

- Fundraising information systems and services, including prospect research, are adequate to support a campaign.

- The development office/foundation has established relationships with such specialists, either internal or external, as may be needed during the campaign—for example, fundraising counsel, planned-giving counsel, and professionals in communications, publications, and event management.

- Adequate budgetary resources have been identified and committed to the campaign.

- There are no or very limited conditions affecting the institution that will have a negative impact on the campaign—for example, recent controversies, internal political divisions, or competing fundraising efforts among units within the campus or a system.

- There are very limited conditions in the external environment—for example, a poor economy or competing campaigns by other organizations in the same state or community—that will have a negative impact on the campaign.

Some of these conditions can, of course, be created as a part of preparing for the campaign. The institution can engage in planning to identify its priorities, hire development staff, engage external advisors, and commit resources to fundraising operations and systems. Other conditions—a weak economy, the presence of competing campaigns, or some event in the life of the institution, such as a recent turnover in the presidency or a key staff position—are mostly relevant for timing of the campaign.

But some circumstances are not controllable, at least in the short term, and may affect the magnitude or the timing of the campaign. If the college or university has a limited pool of prospects—perhaps because of its history, location, or the types of programs it offers—that may cap what is a realistic goal.

Additional prospects may not have been identified yet; some prospects' financial capacity may have been underestimated; others might have the ability to give, but their interest has yet to be fully developed. There may be potential in some of those circumstances. But if such prospects simply do not exist, then the goal of the campaign must be appropriately modest. Otherwise, it represents little more than wishful thinking.

SETTING ACADEMIC PRIORITIES

The preparation for a campaign often begins even before the official counting period—that is, the official time during which gifts and other commitments are credited or counted toward the campaign goal. The process begins when the institution begins its cycle of academic planning. Fundraising in a vacuum (that is, for the simple reason that "we need money") is unlikely to excite anybody and is certain to evoke no more than token responses. Especially in today's world of informed donors, many of whom consider their gifts to be like investments, it is essential to explain how the campaign relates to a broader vision and plan that will advance the college or university toward substantive academic goals.

Academic planning and campaign planning are concurrent and iterative processes. As academic priorities are identified, campaign planning must take them into account. But academic planning also must be influenced by the realities of the philanthropic marketplace, and although some objectives can be met through fundraising, others will require a different strategy. As discussed in Chapter 3, academic planning is a responsibility of the institution and the institution's governing board. But if the foundation is to lead the campaign, then there is a shared responsibility, and the foundation board also must be engaged in the planning process in appropriate ways. If the institution shortchanges the academic planning process and just launches a campaign based on goals set by the development office, foundation staff, or someone else, campaign goals and objectives reflect a mere wish list, and the case for support is unlikely to be compelling.

CAMPAIGN PLANNING

While institutional planning must precede a campaign, much campaign preparation already will be underway concurrently with this broader process. Foundation and institutional-development staff members and resources may be increased, new foundation directors enlisted with an eye to bolstering campaign leadership, prospects researched and rated, and prospective major donors apprised of the institution's planning as it unfolds. As the institutional plan comes into focus, planning for the campaign itself moves into higher gear. In this more directed phase of campaign planning, the pace of preparation intensifies, and the focus shifts from the institution's strategic goals toward tactical planning for the fundraising effort.

Because a campaign is complex and unfolds over a number of years, it is essential to ensure broad understanding of its goals, objectives, and policies. The board that serves at the end of the campaign may be quite different from the board that initiated the campaign years earlier. It is essential that the ground rules—for example, gift-accounting and gift-acceptance policies—remain consistent. It also is especially important to maintain clear policies regarding what types of gifts will be counted and in what manner, and how donors will be recognized. All of that should be considered carefully as a part of campaign planning in order to avoid confusion or misunderstanding along the way.

One area that may elicit discussion is campaign-accounting rules. These delineate how various types of gifts (for example, current and deferred) will be credited toward the goal and how long the campaign will extend in order to reach its stated goal. The CASE campaign guidelines provide a sound basis for such decisions and permit sufficient flexibility for individual institutions to adapt their policies to meet their specific campaign objectives.

Once campaign accounting rules are agreed upon, the foundation board and the wider campus community must clearly understand them. Campaign totals should be transparent, with a clear differentiation among current gifts, pledges, and long-term deferred commitments. That is especially true if the campaign is to include long-term commitments, some of which may even be revocable by the donor. In too many instances, campaigns reach their announced goal only to become targets of criticism and cynicism by those who anticipated the availability of greater current resources—but who then learn that much of the campaign total comprises deferred gifts that will be given later and annual-fund gifts that already have been expended.

As academic and campaign planning begin to converge, a preliminary campaign goal and objectives should be identified, and the market should be tested (perhaps through a feasibility study). After that, the campaign case statement should be drafted, campaign budgets determined, and the key volunteer leaders of the campaign identified and enlisted.

The foundation and the institution will need to decide how the campaign budget is to be financed. Some campaigns are funded through additions to regular operating budgets, some by capitalizing expenses, some through a variety of gift-tax and fee arrangements, some by applying unrestricted gifts to cover costs, or some combination of methods. A full discussion of the subject is beyond the scope of this chapter, but resources are available from CASE on its Web site (www.case.org) that explain the various options for funding a foundation or a campaign. If gift taxes are applied, the board will need to clearly communicate such arrangements to prospective donors.

SETTING CAMPAIGN PRIORITIES, OBJECTIVES, AND GOALS

A major decision in campaign planning is, of course, identifying the amount to be raised and the purposes for which it will be raised—that is, the goal and objectives of the campaign. The vocabulary of campaigns has evolved over time, and some terms are used inconsistently, both among authors and campaigns. That is not necessarily a problem, as long as everyone involved understands what they mean in a specific context. But some further clarity might be helpful.

For example, the terms "goal" and "goals" are used fairly consistently and refer to the dollar totals that the campaign is expected to achieve. There may be an overall goal and then various sub-goals, which may be broken out in various ways. But the *purposes* for which the dollars are being raised have come to be described and presented in different ways over time. In earlier decades they were usually called "needs," and a compilation of them was the "needs list." The term has somewhat of a charitable connotation, and it reflects an internal perspective, but "needs" is still used in some campaigns and in conversations about them.

In the 1990s, the purposes of campaigns came to be identified as "objectives," adopting some of the language and perspective of strategic planning. Some were highlighted as "featured objectives"—those receiving the most emphasis. Objectives are similar to needs in that they are specific purposes, such as endowments for chairs, scholarships, or the construction or renovation of buildings. Both terms—objectives and featured objectives—are still widely used to describe the purposes of campaigns.

Since the 2000s, there has been a trend toward identifying broad campaign "priorities" or "strategic priorities," under which objectives are often organized. Those cross-cutting themes place the campaign in the context of the institution's overall strategy and direction. Some campaign priorities reflect external themes (e.g., "preserving the environment" or "advancing medical knowledge"), and some describe priorities that are more campus-focused (e.g., "advancing undergraduate education" or "strengthening faculty research"). Some campaigns abbreviate the latter and organize campaign goals simply around the priorities of "students," "faculty," and so forth.

Again, the terms "priorities" and "objectives" are not consistently applied within the field. Some campaigns use the terms interchangeably. Some nest objectives within priorities; others, priorities within objectives. Again, that is not necessarily a problem, as long as there is consistency within a particular campaign.

The goals of a comprehensive campaign can be sliced in five basic ways:

- *By the use of the funds.* Those include endowment, capital projects (facilities and equipment), and current use (both unrestricted and restricted). By definition, comprehensive campaigns encompass giving for all of these uses. Gifts, pledges, and, in many cases, planned gift commitments will be credited toward one or another. Some donors will combine the annual fund, an endowment gift, and perhaps support for a building project within a single commitment to the campaign.

- *By priorities.* As an example, there may be a sub-goal of the campaign related to the priority of advancing undergraduate education that subsumes other projects related to the undergraduate experience, such as scholarships or the construction or renovation of a student center or residence halls. A priority of advancing knowledge might encompass endowed chairs and professorships, as well as funds for research, laboratories, or libraries.

- *By unit.* At colleges and universities, defining goals and objectives for each major unit (including colleges and schools, research institutes or centers, and campuswide programs like athletics or student life) helps to harness the leadership of deans and the loyalty that many alumni attach to the college or school where they received their educations. In many comprehensive campaigns, each component of the overall effort operates like a campaign of its own, with volunteer leaders, development staff members, and deans carrying out all of the roles described in Chapter 3 of this book, with overall coordination and direction from the central administration.

- *By objectives.* Some smaller campaigns do not describe cross-cutting themes or priorities. Rather, they go right to specific projects—for example, $10 million for endowed scholarships and $10 million for renovation of the student center.

- *By the impact of commitments.* CASE's campaign-management guidelines encourage institutions to break out the overall campaign goal into separate goals for current and deferred gifts and to maintain the distinction in reporting campaign progress. That helps to avoid misunderstanding about the impact of campaign commitments—some that may be available to the institution immediately and others that may become available only in the future.

Institutions adopt different formats for displaying the goals and purposes of their campaigns. That is acceptable, but it is important to maintain clarity and simplicity. The goals, priorities, and objectives of a well-planned campaign should be consistent when viewed from various perspectives. In other words, they should form a matrix in which the cross-cutting priorities can be spread across academic units or the use of funds with a number in each cell and consistent totals for each row and column.

As examples, Figures 6.2 and 6.3 summarize the campaigns of two public universities: the University of California, Berkeley and the University of Maryland College Park. On its Web site, Berkeley lists the goals by objective, while Maryland presents the campaign according to broader priorities. Drilling down further into either Web site can reveal the goals sliced in other ways, including by academic unit.

Figure 6.2
The Campaign for Berkeley Campaign Goals
(Total campaign goal: $3 billion)

Program support
  Undergraduate education and student life;
  athletic and cultural programs; schools and colleges
	$670,000,000

Facilities	$600,000,000
Research	$450,000,000
Faculty chairs and funds	$390,000,000
Graduate fellowships	$340,000,000
Undergraduate scholarships	$300,000,000
Annual support	$250,000,000

Figure 6.3
Great Expectations: The Campaign for Maryland

Campaign Priorities
(Total campaign goal: $1 billion)

• *Providing students the opportunity to reach for the stars.* (Goal: $350 Million)
The campaign will raise needed funds to: help exceptionally talented students who have low to moderate financial means attend Maryland; significantly enhance the undergraduate experience by providing every freshman the opportunity to engage in a special, extracurricular learning experience that complements the degree program; and position the university to successfully compete for the most talented graduate students.

• *Ensuring our faculty are competitive with the best.* (Goal: $225 Million)
The campaign will raise funds to significantly enhance the university's ability to compete for the world's most talented faculty, and then provide faculty with the intellectual, physical, and financial resources necessary for them to be top lecturers and teachers, win research grants, and be nationally and internationally recognized for their leadership in the disciplines.

• *Creating an environment of excellence.* (Goal: $175 Million)
The campaign will raise the funds that are critically necessary to provide state-of-the-art facilities in which learning, teaching, research, and artistic and athletic performance can flourish. Funds will also assure a physical setting across campus and in adjacent areas that is vibrant, visually appealing, pedestrian-friendly, and environmentally sensitive.

• *Supporting innovation to change the world around us.* (Goal: $250 Million)
The campaign will raise needed funds to stimulate "big ideas" and support entrepreneurial programs and innovation, as well as provide the flexible venture funding that enables the university and its schools, colleges, and programs to act quickly and seize new opportunities.

CAMPAIGN DECISION MAKERS

Establishing the campaign goal, priorities, and objectives is an essential task in the planning phase of the campaign. But who makes those decisions? The 2010 AGB survey provided data regarding the influence of various players in setting such goals and objectives. Similar data were obtained in a study conducted by AGB in 2000 and reported in *A Board's Guide to Comprehensive Campaigns* (AGB Press), edited by Jake B. Schrum; those data were also based on a survey of public colleges and universities. So it is possible to compare results to identify patterns and possible trends.

The results of the two studies are not entirely comparable. Institutions were asked to identify the three individuals or groups who were most influential in 2000, and they were asked to identify the four most influential in 2010. The 2010 survey included the foundation board's development committee and outside consultants as explicit response options, but the 2000 survey did not. However, general patterns are observable in the summary presented in Table 6.2:

Table 6.2
Influence on Campaign Goals and Objectives

(Percentage of respondents citing the following as one of top 3 or 4)

	2000 AGB survey (top 3 influential)	2010 AGB survey (top 4 influential)
Campaign leadership committee	13.1%	54.7%
Chief academic officer of the institution	23.2%	24.5%
Chief advancement officer/foundation chief executive	33.8%	20.8%
External consultant	Not asked	39.6%
Faculty committee	11.6%	5.7%
Foundation board as a whole	27.3%	41.5%
Foundation board chair	3.0%	20.8%
Foundation board's development or fundraising committee	Not asked	17.0%
Fundraising/development committee of the institutional governing board	1.5%	11.3%
Institution chief executive	71.2%	88.7%
Institution's governing board	16.7%	24.5%
Other committees of the institutional governing board	1.0%	1.9%
Other individuals/groups	5.1%	11.3%

The top three individuals or groups mentioned in 2010 were the institution's chief executive, the campaign leadership committee, and the foundation board. The top three mentioned in 2000 were the institution's chief executive, the institution's chief advancement officer, and the foundation board. The data suggest that the president or chancellor remains a dominant figure in establishing goals and objectives, and that perhaps there is now a somewhat larger role for the campaign leadership committee, a structure that has become more common within the past decade. The campaign leadership committee will be discussed further later in this chapter.

Table 6.2 shows that consultants now play a significant role in the planning of many campaigns. A board may need to consider whether to engage outside campaign counsel. It used to be common for institutions to contract with a consulting firm to bring a professional to the campus for a period of months or years—not to actually raise funds, but to organize, manage, and direct campaign activity. They were known as "resident campaign managers." Today, most colleges and universities have seasoned staff professionals, and that old model of campaign consulting has all but disappeared.

Consultants today are widely engaged for two purposes. First, as I mentioned previously, in many situations a feasibility study is desirable during campaign planning. The objectivity of an outside consultant is helpful in gauging whether the proposed goal and campaign objectives are realistic. Moreover, in the feasibility study, people are asked to think about the institution and its needs, making the process a way to help cultivate potential major donors. When an institution engages a consultant to conduct a study, it signals to key constituents that the campaign is something new and big, and thus requires a more thoughtful response than the institution's regular, ongoing fundraising.

Results of the feasibility study should inform the campaign planning and may result in revisions to the preliminary goal or the priorities of the campaign before the quiet phase of solicitation is launched. Thus it is not surprising that consultants are considered to be among the important influences on what goals and priorities are ultimately adopted.

In addition to the consultant's support in campaign planning, periodic consulting throughout the campaign also can be helpful and is common. A consultant who meets on a regular basis with the foundation CEO and/or chief advancement officer, other development staff, the president, the development committee, and the campaign leadership committee can provide an objective and experienced voice and help bridge any differences that may arise at critical points during the campaign.

During the period of campaign planning, it is essential to set goals for each of the institution's major constituencies, including the foundation board. Regardless of whether the board has a policy requiring a minimum annual gift, a campaign is a special situation that calls for a tailored approach. It is simply a reality that a campaign cannot succeed unless the board collectively produces an adequate portion of the goal through its own gifts. Moreover, board commitments during the campaign's quiet period can make or break the campaign at the outset. A long-standing rule of thumb is that the board generally must give from 20 to 25 percent of the total campaign goal, but some institutions more recently have revised that number higher. In the 2010 AGB survey, which included a variety of institutional types, foundation chief executives reported that foundation board gifts accounted for an average of 18.4 percent of total gifts to their campaigns.

How much should board members give? The right answer depends, of course, on the size and scope of the institution's constituency and the types of gifts the campaign will encompass. For example, at a research university, where research grants may be counted as part of the campaign, board gifts may be a smaller percentage than they must be at a small college or community college with a more limited constituency and perhaps fewer opportunities to secure significant corporate and foundation support.

THE QUIET (OR SILENT) PHASE

Once a decision has been made to mount a campaign, institutions still have a long way to go before reserving a hall for the kickoff event and sending out tweets about the campaign. It is time to begin quietly soliciting support from board members and those at the top of the prospect list.

The concept of "sequential fundraising," a term introduced by the late George A. Brakeley Jr., a highly regarded consultant, applies in this phase of the campaign. It means that gifts are solicited, as Brakeley described it, "from the top down and the inside out." In other words, the top prospects are solicited first in order to set sights for others, and insiders are solicited before moving on to less involved constituencies, like the general alumni body or the local community.

The terms "quiet phase" and "silent phase" are both used to describe this period in the campaign, sometimes interchangeably (even by me). But I think "quiet phase" is probably more accurate and helps to alleviate what is sometimes a point of misunderstanding. Of course, there will be many people who know about the campaign during this stage. All members of both the foundation board and the institutional governing board will know. The administration will know, as will many members of the faculty and staff. So, too, will people who may have been interviewed in the feasibility study, and, surely, those who have been approached for leadership gifts.

So the campaign is not totally silent. But it is quiet in the sense that the institution has made no public announcement and not generally publicized the details—including the campaign goal—although they may be widely rumored. Indeed, it is best to cultivate some air of uncertainty, even mystery, about the progress of the quiet phase and what goal may ultimately be announced. Doing so helps to maintain interest and build excitement and momentum.

Money committed during the quiet phase will constitute the nucleus fund, the amount of which will be announced at the time of the campaign kickoff. Such gifts typically constitute a significant portion of the total campaign—perhaps one-half or more. It is essential to resist going public with the campaign during the quiet period. Doing so may reduce the motivation of the best prospects to make exceptional commitments that can inspire other donors; instead, publicity may cause them to make gifts that are less thoughtful and considered. The result can be a lowering of expectations throughout the donor base and a campaign that is doomed even as it leaves the gate. Board leaders must stand strong against any urging—from within their own ranks or outside—to prematurely announce a campaign until a sufficient nucleus fund has been achieved.

Looking back at Table 6.1, in 2010 the average nucleus fund exceeded 50 percent of the final goal at all institution types, except for two-year institutions. That number is generally consistent with other studies, including AGB's 2004 study of campaigns at independent colleges and universities. A 2000 AGB survey of *public* college and university campaigns, reported in *A Board's Guide to Comprehensive Campaigns* (AGB Press), found that an average of 42.7 percent of the overall goal had been raised in the quiet phase. Thus, the nucleus fund appears to account for a somewhat larger portion of the campaign today than a decade ago, probably reflecting the increased importance of the top gifts to overall campaign results. Then and now, this phase of the campaign is critical to campaign success.

There is no question that the foundation board's universal participation in the nucleus fund is essential in campaigns for public colleges and universities. Foundation directors also are quite likely to be among the leadership donors whose exceptional commitments set the tone for all other donors. Foundation CEOs responding to the 2010 AGB survey said that gifts from foundation board members totaled, on average, 22.2 percent of the nucleus fund. That compares to 20.7 percent in the study of public-institution campaigns conducted by AGB a decade earlier—not much change. Compared with the independent colleges and universities surveyed by AGB in 2004, both percentages are low. In that 2004 study, trustees of independent institutions had given an average of 35 percent of the campaign's nucleus fund. Of course, public institutions may have two boards that are relevant to the campaign—the foundation board and the institutional governing board. However, foundation chief executives in 2010 reported that gifts from the institutional governing board played a relatively small role in giving, either to the nucleus fund or to the campaign overall. Governing board members provided just 2.9 percent of the average nucleus fund and 2.7 percent of the average total given to the campaign.

Who solicits gifts to the nucleus fund? The 2010 AGB survey posed that question to foundation chief executives, producing the results summarized in Table 6.3.

Table 6.3
Solicitors of Gifts to Campaign Nucleus Fund
(Foundation CEOs checked "all that apply")

Institution president	84.0%
Foundation CEO	76.0%
Institution's chief advancement officer or advancement staff	72.0%
Foundation board chair	68.0%
Other foundation board members	58.0%
Members of special campaign leadership committee	52.0%
Members of the foundation board development committee	30.0%
Governing board chair	22.0%
Development committee of the governing board	10.0%
Executive committee of the governing board	8.0%

Table 6.3 reveals the significant role played by the institution's president and the foundation board chair in the quiet phase of the campaign. Both parties participate in solicitations in the overwhelming majority of cases. This is understandable since commitments solicited in the early years of a campaign are leadership gifts solicited from board members, previous major donors, and other top prospects. The involvement of the institution's president and foundation board chair will usually be essential to influence the decisions of such important donors. Another interesting fact revealed by the data in Table 6.3 is the important role played by foundation CEOs and institutional chief advancement officers (the same person about half the time) in the solicitation of important leadership gifts. The survey was not designed to determine how often one of them participated in a solicitation together with the institution's president or foundation board chair, but we can assume that a team approach is common. Interestingly, the foundation chief executives report that almost a quarter of governing board chairs participated as solicitors in the quiet phase of campaigns, despite the fact that gifts from governing board members were not a significant portion of the nucleus fund or the overall campaign. And again the data suggest an important role for members of the campaign leadership committee, which I will discuss further later in this chapter.

THE KICKOFF

Once the nucleus fund has been obtained, it is time to make a public announcement of the campaign, its goal and objectives, the total amount achieved, and the lead gifts that have been committed during the quiet phase. The institution will recognize the leadership donors and highlight the campaign volunteers at what is usually one of the most elaborate public events that it will mount. That begins the public phase of the campaign, a term that may encompass several stages.

Some observers point to the risk of a "plateau of fatigue" occurring right after the kickoff, when the energy expended in the quiet period and in preparation for the kickoff event leads to a burnout that can reduce the campaign's momentum. If that occurs, the president, chief advancement officer, foundation CEO, and foundation board must provide leadership to sustain campaign enthusiasm.

THE PUBLIC PHASE

Eventually the campaign expands outward in concentric circles to donors who are less engaged with the institution and whose gift capabilities are at successively lower levels. Some authors describe a "general gifts phase," in which the institution conducts broad-based mail and phone solicitations for the campaign. But most comprehensive campaigns today include the annual fund, which covers that segment of the market. Comprehensive campaign solicitations usually stay focused on major gifts. Depending on the distribution of the institution's constituency, the campaign also may encompass regional campaigns.

The closing months of the public phase are sometimes called the "cleanup" phase. This period includes an intensive effort to reach the goal by the deadline. It may involve revisiting donor prospects who were approached earlier in the campaign but who were not then ready to make a commitment. It may include solicitations of prospects who were identified during the campaign and only now are prepared to give. And in some circumstances, the closing phase may require returning to donors who already have made commitments in order to ask for increased support.

The final year or months of a comprehensive campaign also may encompass special efforts focused on particular projects or categories of donors. It may be that new priorities and needs have been identified by the institution in the years since the campaign was launched. New deans may have arrived with new agendas, or new programs may have been developed that can attract donors who were previously not interested.

THE VICTORY CELEBRATION

The campaign concludes with a celebration of victory, often a major event that rivals the kickoff in its scale. This is an opportunity to honor donors, volunteers, and everyone who has played a role in the effort. It can be a magical occasion in which the entire campus community can feel pride in a great achievement and a leap forward for their institution.

Most campaigns achieve their overall dollar goals, although it is important for foundation directors and everyone else to understand that comprehensive campaigns may be successful without achieving every goal related to each specific objective. Two realities come into play.

First, many college and university campaigns extend over long periods—often as long as eight years. No matter how carefully planned, a campaign's conditions may evolve. Economic conditions may change, donor interests and attitudes may change, or the institution may have new leadership with different priorities. It is not unusual, for example, for a comprehensive campaign to achieve its overall dollar goal and meet its goals for current operating support and endowment, but fall short on gifts toward new facilities. Or perhaps one unit of a university has just missed its goal while others have exceeded theirs. This is not an ideal outcome, of course, but it does not imply an unsuccessful campaign if the overall goal has been reached. Rather, it may suggest a strategy for the post-campaign period, perhaps repackaging unmet campaign objectives in a series of more-focused fundraising efforts.

Second, foundation directors should keep in mind that a comprehensive campaign is as much a communications strategy for the institution as it is a fundraising methodology. Achieving the overall campaign goal is a victory worthy of visible and enthusiastic celebration. Success breeds success. Support flows to institutions perceived as "on the move." People support winners. The positive psychology of a successful campaign is important to future donors' perceptions of the college or university, as well as to those of prospective students, peer institutions that vote in reputational surveys, and other constituencies. The campaign victory celebration is an important vehicle for positioning and advancing the institution and should be given as much emphasis as the institution can afford. Again, certain components of a comprehensive campaign may fall short, but that does not diminish the achievement of reaching the overall campaign goal. It just sets the agenda for future fundraising, which must be continuous, regardless of whether the institution is involved in a formal campaign.

Although the victory celebration marks the official conclusion of the campaign, there is yet another phase. It is essential to study and analyze the campaign to determine the lessons learned and any unmet needs that should become the priorities of post-campaign fundraising. New leaders and prospects will have been identified in the course of the campaign, and institutions need to plan for their continued engagement and affiliation—perhaps developing the top leadership for the next campaign.

CAMPAIGN LEADERSHIP

The volunteer leaders are vital to the success of a campaign, not only for what they do, but also because of who they are. The reputations of those who hold positions as campaign chairs, vice chairs, committee chairs, and so forth bring credibility to the campaign and signify its importance to the institution. Because they are in leadership positions, foundation directors must be highly visible among this group.

The most common approach to organizing campaign leadership is the creation of a special committee, which may be called the "campaign leadership committee," "campaign cabinet," "campaign steering committee," or some other name.

In the 2010 AGB survey, 69.2 percent of foundation CEOs reported that their campaigns were led by a special campaign committee. For another 15.4 percent, campaign leadership was provided by the foundation board; for 11.5 percent, the campaign leadership group was the foundation board's development committee; and, for 3.8 percent of campaigns, the leadership group was the development committee of the institution's governing board. Those data reflect significant change from 2000, when another study by AGB found that only 33 percent of public institutions had created a separate campaign leadership group, and from a 2003 study, also conducted by AGB, that found separate campaign committees at 50 percent of the public institutions that were surveyed. In AGB's 2004 study of independent colleges and universities, 72 percent reported having a separate campaign committee, so this has become common practice across the sectors.

Why? Foundation CEOs were asked to explain in the 2010 AGB survey and their answers are summarized in Table 6.4.

Table 6.4
Reasons for Creating a Separate Campaign Leadership Committee
(Foundation chief executives were asked to check "all that apply")

To recruit campaign leadership from outside the foundation board	68.3%
To keep the foundation board as a whole focused on funds management, general strategy, and policy	29.3%
To ensure the involvement of both governing board and foundation board members	22.0%
For political reasons within the foundation or the institution	12.2%
There were not enough members of the foundation board or the governing board who were able to raise funds.	9.8%

A separate campaign committee offers many advantages. Thinking back to the earlier discussion of the foundation board's larger responsibilities for the management of funds, it may not be desirable to distract the entire board with campaign matters, nor to distract the campaign's leaders by the foundation's larger agenda. Creating a separate campaign leadership committee is a way to bring both the foundation board and the institutional governing board together in a common effort, helping to ensure that the campaign is well communicated and understood by both bodies.

The campaign committee also provides a vehicle for enlisting the participation of people beyond the foundation and institutional governing boards in guiding important elements of the campaign. For example, there may be regional campaign committees with chairs who also need to be represented on the overall campaign leadership committee. And it is common for such outside members of this committee to become visible as potential future board members, providing a pipeline of people who have proved their commitment and effectiveness through participation in the campaign.

The campaign leadership committees described by foundation CEOs include members of both the foundation and institution boards, with foundation board members the predominant number. But committees also include institutional officers like the president, vice president, and deans; alumni who are not board members; and some parents. A campaign committee may be one of the most representative groups ever assembled to work in common purpose to advance the college or university. The benefits of its work go beyond campaign success; the shared effort and responsibility can be important in building the institution's larger culture and a tradition of achievement and pride.

The campaign approach has some critics. Some will argue that a campaign forces fundraising on the institution's timetable, rather than in accordance with the life stages and financial positions of donors or in sync with each individual's developing relationship with the college or university. They would argue for a continuous program of major and planned gifts that is donor-centered and that gives greater priority to the interests and inclinations of the givers. But there is no evidence that colleges and universities are abandoning the campaign approach; indeed, campaign goals continue to increase. During the economic downturn that began in 2007 and its aftermath, some colleges and universities held back on announcing new campaigns, and others were challenged to complete those that were already in progress. But many wisely used the recession as a time to secure relationships, focus on planned giving, enhance annual fund programs, and plan—quietly—for the launch of a new campaign once the environment improved.

Today's campaigns are marketing as well as fundraising strategies. They are vehicles for bringing visibility and excitement to the institution's achievements as well as its goals across a broad range of activities. It seems likely that comprehensive campaigns will continue to be the primary advancement strategy of colleges and universities for the foreseeable future—and thus a central focus of foundation directors in exercising their fundraising responsibilities.

VOICES FROM THE FIELD

Representative comments from foundation chief executives regarding the foundation board in a campaign:

"Our board members were very engaged in planning and then solicitation while we were in a campaign. Now they are complacent and in need of a rest."

"It is important to have a strategic and well-planned campaign with a plan of action that reaches out far enough for the board members to see and understand the importance of their role."

"The foundation executive needs to partner with the foundation board chair and the campaign committee chair to set and deliver on goals. Need very specific plans and follow up."

"Members of the foundation board executive committee were especially important in making larger campaign gifts. A few key members made a difference by opening doors and soliciting campaign gifts."

"Board members need to embrace the mission of the institution and understand the campaign initiatives and case for support. Only some have the potential to participate in fundraising. The CEO needs to use their time wisely and coordinate with them."

"Because we are in a campaign the board is evolving toward being more active and hands-on."

Questions for Foundation Boards to Consider

- Before launching a campaign, has the board ensured that the effort will be based on sound institutional plans, fundraising goals, and objectives that reflect institutional priorities?

- Has the board determined that the proposed campaign goal is realistic? Has a feasibility study been completed? Is one needed?

- Has the board discussed policy questions, including the length of the campaign, the types of gifts to count and in what manner, and the types of gifts to accept? And how will donors be recognized?

- Do all trustees understand the level of giving that will be required from the board? Has the board determined if it is willing and able to give at this level?

- Has the board considered the advantages of creating a separate campaign leadership committee on which foundation board members would play important roles?

- Is there a clear, written understanding between the institution and the foundation regarding their respective roles and responsibilities to approve the priorities and goals of the campaign and to support the campaign?

- Does the foundation understand the budgetary-resource requirements for the proposed campaign and have the capacity to provide incremental funds if necessary?

CASE STUDY

PLANNING AND LEADING A CAMPAIGN:
UNIVERSITY OF CONNECTICUT FOUNDATION

The University of Connecticut Foundation, founded in 1964, serves as the primary fundraising arm for the main campus in Storrs, five regional campuses, the schools of law and social work, a graduate business learning center, and the schools of medicine and dental medicine at the UConn Health Center. John K. Martin was appointed president of the foundation in 2003, having previously served as vice chancellor for advancement at the University System of Maryland and president and chief executive officer of the University of Maryland Foundation.

The UConn Foundation completed a campaign in 2004, raising $325 million. Intensive planning for a new campaign began just two years later. The new campaign, "Our University, Our Moment," was announced in 2009 with a goal of $600 million after raising $190 million in the quiet phase.

Preparation for the new campaign began when the university's provost and deans initiated an academic strategic planning process, with encouragement from the foundation's board of directors. The foundation board was involved in responding to the academic priorities that emerged from the planning and ensuring that the campaign's overarching goals and timeline would be attainable.

Once the academic priorities were identified by the university's academic leaders, the foundation worked to identify specific fundraising targets and objectives. Through extensive discussions with academic leaders, the foundation developed specific breakdowns for areas of support, wrote case statements, and identified the resources needed to carry out the campaign. The final goals and priorities were eventually approved by both the university leadership and the foundation's board of directors.

Oversight of the campaign is provided by a campaign steering committee, led by a former chair and current member of the foundation board. The committee includes current and former foundation directors and other donors and volunteers. The foundation board's development committee also reviews campaign progress and makes recommendations concerning specific fundraising programs. A larger group, the National Development Council, was formed in 2008 to broaden the base of volunteers. Members of the council provide personal giving, help identify donor prospects, and assist in the solicitation of gifts.

Martin emphasizes the vital role that was played by the foundation board in planning and launching the campaign. The planning phase took place during a difficult period for the national economy as well as turnover in the university's leadership, including two presidents and a number of deans.

"We are a relatively young fundraising operation," Martin says, "and this was a challenging undertaking. Providing continuity and forward progress under such circumstances is an example of the leadership a foundation board can help provide to the university. The foundation's focus is entirely on building a self-sustaining fundraising organization that will help to elevate UConn among the top tier of national universities. We take pride that the foundation is moving private support to the forefront."

CHAPTER 7

STRIVING FOR BEST PRACTICE

As I wrote in Chapter 1, the 2010 AGB survey on the fundraising role of boards of institutionally related foundations was mostly about what is—that is, it collected data that describe the current state of affairs regarding the involvement of foundation boards in fundraising. It was not designed principally to identify best practices of foundation boards or foundation chief executive officers. Throughout the book, I have offered my own opinions on various subjects and have cited, or at least invoked, the advice of others who have written on the topic. Foundation CEOs who responded to AGB's survey also offered suggestions, but of course, what works in one setting may not be universally applicable. In sum, the data provided through the AGB survey do not *directly* support any recommendations of universal best practices.

Also, defining best practices can be problematic. It is often challenging to define or measure effective fundraising in a way that reflects all of the variables—institutional history, location, culture, alumni and community demographics, mix of programs, and more—that significantly influence the ultimate bottom line of how much money the foundation or the institution raises to meet its needs and address its goals.

Indeed, one reality that is evident from the responses is the great variety of situations found at different institutions and foundations. Some foundations remain primarily fiduciary entities that manage but do not raise funds. Others are in the process of evolving from fund managers to active fundraising organizations. Their boards vary in their understanding and ability to engage in active fundraising. And some foundations are highly functioning, in multiple roles, with foundation directors deeply engaged in raising significant private support.

In the 2010 AGB survey, CEOs of foundations were asked to provide a brief description, in their own words, of the role that their foundation board plays in fundraising. A few representative comments illustrate both the range of current circumstances—along a noticeable continuum from passive to active—as well as the evolution that is underway:

"Our board is very passive."

"Our board is more advisory and less active in pursuing gifts."

"The board does not give a priority to fundraising."

"The foundation board has tremendous potential but has not achieved that potential."

"Our foundation directors have a growing sense of their responsibilities."

"Currently, the board is involved in personal giving, but we are in the process of educating them about their role in fundraising."

"The board is becoming more effective. Some members are very involved; others are just beginning to get involved."

"The foundation board is maturing into one that has an expectation of giving, cultivating, and soliciting gifts."

"Our board members are active, willing to introduce new leads, will go on visits when asked, and are willing to follow up with calls and letters."

"Foundation board members are actively engaged in the identification, cultivation, and solicitation of private gifts to the institution."

"Our board provides leadership in the fundraising process, supported by the staff."

TAKEAWAYS FOR FOUNDATION BOARD MEMBERS

- **Universal best practices for foundation fundraising can be difficult to determine, as they often depend on variables like the institution's location or the demographics of its alumni and other potential donors.**

- **Some key themes that emerged in the AGB 2010 survey were, among others, that foundation directors should make personal gift commitments and set explicit goals for overall board performance.**

- **By helping to raise funds for their institutions, foundation boards can make major contributions to higher education, which in turn shapes the lives of millions of students and ensures America's economic future.**

All this is not to say that foundation boards, foundation executives, and chief advancement officers cannot or should not establish specific measures of performance and be accountable for them. They should and they must. Rather, the point is that performance metrics—and best practices—often need to be determined in the specific context of an institution. The experience and advice of others provide a guide, but need to be adapted to the realities and circumstances of each institution and its foundation.

FOUNDATION BOARD BEST PRACTICES

With those caveats, however, foundation chief executives who participated in the 2010 AGB survey were offered the opportunity to submit open-ended suggestions of best practices. Their responses reveal some clear patterns. The CEOs were asked to identify, in their own words, "the one most important practice for the foundation board itself to ensure that it is effective in fundraising." The responses reflect common themes, none of which are surprising because they are consistent with much of what has been written and stated by most experts who have considered the topic. Those themes include:

- Have a commitment to the institution, its mission, and priorities.
- Understand the case for private support.
- Recruit other directors with the capacity to give and engage in fundraising and be clear about expectations from the beginning.
- Set explicit goals and expectations for board performance, engage in board self-assessment, and hold directors accountable.
- Make personal gift commitments.
- Work as partners with the staff in identifying, cultivating, and soliciting prospects.

Some foundation executives offered specific recommendations consistent with these points, including:

"Develop a board evaluation tool that includes activities associated with the fundraising process."

"Provide strong leadership from the chair and the executive committee."

"Make assignments and hold regular report meetings so there is accountability for making the calls."

"Hold fundraising training sessions for the board."

BEST PRACTICES FOR FOUNDATION CHIEF EXECUTIVES

Another reality revealed by AGB's study is the central role played by foundation chief executive officers. Of course, as noted earlier in this book, foundation CEOs were the respondents to the survey, and their comments might be expected to reflect their particular perspective.

The complexity of the foundation CEO's job is evident. He or she is often the link between the institution and the foundation—whether he or she also serves as an institutional officer or not—and between the foundation board and the institution's chief executive. It is a position that offers the opportunity for great impact on public higher education, but one that also requires generous quantities of judgment and skill.

What is "the one most important practice for the foundation CEO to ensure that the board is effective in fundraising?" Again, the executives' responses in their own words follow some common themes:

- Communicate and keep the board informed through personal communications, both with individual board members and the full board.
- Influence the recruitment of new foundation directors with the capacity to give and engage in fundraising.
- Provide opportunities for the board to become educated, both about the institution and fundraising.
- Provide opportunities for the board to be engaged in the life of the institution and its programs.
- Recognize directors who give or make an effort in fundraising.
- Utilize board members; ask them to do something specific.
- Set clear metrics for fundraising success and report on progress.
- Lead by example in terms of commitment to the institution and the foundation.

Some foundation executives offered specific recommendations consistent with these points, including:

"Dog them, thank them, stroke them, and support them."

"Find one or two board members who can be used as examples, finding even the smallest successes and complimenting directors for taking steps in asking."

"Help the board see the ways they can help us be most effective—celebrate successes with them when they help us identify, cultivate, and close a gift."

"Have regular individual meetings with board members to remind them of the importance of their role in fundraising and invite them to join foundation/institution staff in fundraising meetings."

"The CEO must articulate and communicate the impact the foundation is making upon the institution with their gifts. This can be done at foundation meetings and privately. The CEO must encourage the foundation board to get involved with fundraising and make them comfortable with the process. The CEO must also recognize who can be effective in fundraising and who brings other talents and treasures."

And, finally, I must report my favorite response to the question, which surely came from a foundation chief executive who was just having a bad day: "I don't know. ... I've tried everything I can think of!"

BUILDING FOUNDATIONS FOR THE FUTURE

As described in Chapter 1, the landscape for public higher education is rapidly changing. It is unlikely that conditions will ever again return to those of earlier decades, in which public appropriations were generally adequate to support the missions of most public institutions while keeping tuition within the reach of most students. Private support and the institutionally related foundations that raise and steward those funds for the benefit of their institutions and society are central to ensuring academic excellence, educational opportunity, and indeed, the future vitality of the nation.

More than 20 years ago, in a book titled *Successful Fundraising for Higher Education* (American Council on Education, 1997), the former president of Cornell University, Frank H.T. Rhodes, wrote words that still provide a contemporary message:

> *The advancement of learning—Francis Bacon's phrase—is the most critical need of our nation. Only learning—and the discovery, skill, knowledge, understanding, insight, enlightenment, and wisdom it embodies—will provide a secure foundation for our well-being.... The health of our people, the strength of our economy, the preservation of our environment, the sustainability of our resources, the defense of our borders, the quality of our daily lives, the civic virtue of our society, the strength of our democracy: all these ultimately depend on the advancement of learning....*
>
> *The successful advancement of learning will require new approaches and new partnerships. It will not be enough to leave the task to teachers and professors, to entrust it to state governors or local school boards, or to rely on presidential initiative or national summits. It must be everybody's business, everyone's concern; it will require a nationwide coalition, a social compact, an intergenerational partnership.... Fundraising is a vital part of this partnership because it facilitates initiative and supports activity, and because it encourages other more active forms of personal engagement and individual leadership.*

The people who serve on boards of institutionally related foundations have accepted positions of great responsibility. But they are also privileged to play such a central role in meeting one of the great challenges of our time. They have an opportunity that few others can share—to have a meaningful impact on the future of important institutions that shape the lives of millions.

That privilege brings an obligation to give and help secure resources. This book has examined the role of foundation directors in what may seem like purely transactional— and perhaps to some, even crass—activities: cultivating relationships, soliciting gifts, setting fundraising goals, and ensuring fundraising success. But it is not all about money, and members of foundation boards should approach their work with a sense of larger purpose. To quote Rhodes again,

> To solicit funds [for a college or university] is not to go cap-in-hand, begging for support for some marginal activity. It is instead, to invite a friend to share in the privilege of the greatest partnership of all—the quest for knowledge, on which our present existence and our future well-being depend.

REFERENCES AND RESOURCES

Association of Governing Boards of Universities and Colleges. *Effective Foundation Boards*. Washington, DC: 2011.

Association of Governing Boards of Universities and Colleges and the Council for Advancement and Support of Education. *Illustrative Memorandum of Understanding Between a Foundation and Host Institution or System*. Washington, DC: 2003.

Association of Governing Boards of Universities and Colleges. [Survey of foundation chief executive officers]. Unpublished survey data. 2010.

Bass, David and James Lanier, "What Lies Ahead for University-Foundation Relations?" *Trusteeship*, November/December 2008.

Boverini, Luisa, "When Venture Philanthropy Rocks the Ivory Tower," *International Journal of Educational Advancement*, February 2006.

Bloom, Gary, "Working Toward a Working Foundation Board," *Trusteeship*, July/August 2008.

Chait, Richard, "The Gremlins of Governance," *Trusteeship*, July/August 2009.

Council for Advancement and Support of Education. *CASE Campaign Report 2007*. Washington, DC: 2007.

Council for Advancement and Support of Education. Flahaven, Brian, preparer. *Institutionally Related Foundations and the Economic Downturn: Results of the 2009 CASE Survey on Foundation Funding Sources and Budget Restructuring*. [CASE white paper.] Washington, DC: 2009.

Council for Aid to Education. *Voluntary Support of Education*. Washington, DC: 2011.

Evans, Gary. *Board Basics: The Development Committee*. Washington, DC: Association of Governing Boards of Universities and Colleges, 2003.

Frohnmayer, Dave, "Trust in the Balance," *Trusteeship*, September/October 2006.

Garland, James, "Rethinking Reform," *Currents*, July/August 2010.

"Great Expectations: The Campaign for Maryland," University of Maryland, accessed March 7, 2011, http://www.greatexpectations.umd.edu/priorities.html.

Hedgepeth, Royster C. *How Public College and University Foundation Boards Contribute to Campaign Success*. Washington, DC: Association of Governing Boards of Universities and Colleges, 2003.

Ingram, Richard T., "Just Ask," *Currents*, March 2004.

Johnson, Nicholas; Phil Oliff; and Erica Williams, "An Update on State Budget Cuts At Least 46 States Have Imposed Cuts That Hurt Vulnerable Residents and the Economy," Web site of the Center for Budget and Policy Priorities, last modified on February 9, 2011. http://www.cbpp.org/cms/index.cfm?fa=view&id=1214.

Kelderman, Eric, "State Lawmakers Seek More Say Over Colleges," *The Chronicle of Higher Education*, March 4, 2011.

Legon, Richard D., ed. *Margin of Excellence: The New Work of Higher Education Foundations*. Washington, DC: Association of Governing Boards of Universities and Colleges, 2005.

Lopez-Rivera, Marisa, "Updates on Capital Campaigns at 43 Colleges and Universities," *The Chronicle of Higher Education*, June 7, 2010.

National Association of State Universities and Land Grant Colleges (now the Association of Public and Land-Grant Universities). *Margin for Excellence: The Role of Voluntary Support in Public Higher Education*. Washington, DC: 1966.

Phelan, Joseph F. *College and University Foundations: Serving America's Public Higher Education*. Washington, DC: Association of Governing Boards of Universities and Colleges, 1997.

Pocock, J.W. *Fundraising Leadership: A Guide for University and College Boards*. Washington, DC: Association of Governing Boards of Universities and Colleges, 1989.

Pulley, John, "Low Water Mark," *Currents*, July/August 2010.

Rhodes, Frank H.T. *Successful Fundraising for Higher Education*. Washington, DC: American Council on Education, 1997.

Rosso, Henry A. *Achieving Excellence in Fund-Raising*. San Francisco: Jossey-Bass, 1991.

Schrum, Jake B., ed. *A Board's Guide to Comprehensive Campaigns*. Washington, DC: Association of Governing Boards of Universities and Colleges, 2000.

Seymour, Harold J. *Designs for Fund-Raising* (2nd ed.). Ambler, PA: Fund-Raising Institute, 1988.

State Higher Education Executive Officers. *State Higher Education Finance: FY 2009*. Washington, DC: SHEEO, 2010.

Steger, Charles W., "Overcome the Emotional Costs of Paying for Fund-Raising," *Trusteeship*, May/June 2000.

The Campaign for Berkeley Web site, accessed March 6, 2011, http://campaign.berkeley.edu/learn-more/goals.cfm.

Thrush, Diane Webber, "The Giving Gap," *Currents*, July/August 2010.

University of Virgina. *Funding the University 2008-2009: A Public-Private Partnership*. Charlottesville, VA: University of Virginia, 2009.

Worth, Michael J. *Securing the Future: A Fundraising Guide for Boards of Independent Colleges and Universities*. Washington, DC: Association of Governing Boards of Universities and Colleges, 2005.

Worth, Michael J. *Sounding Boards: Advisory Council in Higher Education*. Washington, DC: Association of Governing Boards of Universities and Colleges, 2008.

ABOUT THE AUTHOR

Michael J. Worth is a professor of nonprofit management at the Trachtenberg School of Public Policy and Public Administration at George Washington University in Washington, D.C. He is also principal of Michael J. Worth & Associates, LLC, a Washington-based consulting firm that advises educational institutions and nonprofit organizations on fundraising strategies and programs.

Worth has more than 35 years of experience in higher education and philanthropic resource development. He served as vice president for development and alumni affairs at George Washington University for almost 20 years and previously served as director of development at the University of Maryland at College Park. At George Washington, he planned and directed two major campaigns and provided support to the board of trustees for board-development programs. Earlier in his career he was director of development at DeSales University and assistant to the president at Wilkes University, both in Pennsylvania.

In addition to numerous articles and reviews, he has written or edited nine books related to fundraising, philanthropy, and board development, including *Securing the Future*, published by AGB in 2005; *Sounding Boards: Advisory Councils in Higher Education*, published by AGB in 2008; and *Leading the Campaign*, published by the American Council on Education in 2010.

He holds a B.A. in economics from Wilkes College, an M.A. in economics from American University, and a Ph.D. in higher education from the University of Maryland.